Dan Leathers

Bill Blowers

D1449848

PUBLISHED BY WINSTON-DEREK PUBLISHERS
Nashville, Tennessee 37205

Library of Congress Cataloging in Publication Data

Johnston, Maury.
   Gays under grace

   Bibliography: p.
   Includes index.
      1.   Homosexuality—Religious aspects—Christianity.
2.   Fundamentalism.   I Title.
   BR115. H6J63 1982   241'.66   82-51217
      ISBN 0-938232-20-7

First Edition

Designer: Marjorie Staton

Printed in the United States of America
10   9   8   7   6   5   4   3   2   1

   ISBN 0-938232-20-7

TO BILL

whose presence in my life
transformed a dream into reality

"For you are not under the law, but under grace."

—The Apostle Paul
Romans 6:14

ACKNOWLEDGMENTS

Grateful acknowledgment is made to all publishers for permission to reprint copyrighted materials. However, this permission does not necessarily imply agreement with the opinions expressed in this book.

Those noted NEB are from The New English Bible. © the Delegates of the Oxford University Press and the Syndics of the Cambridge University Press 1961, 1970. Reprinted by permission.

Those noted CLNT are from the Concordant Literal New Testament, Copyright © 1926, 1931, 1944, 1966 by Concordant Publishing Concern. Used by permission.

Those noted NIV are from The Holy Bible: New International Version. Copyright © 1973 by The New York Bible Society International. Used by permission.

Those noted JB are from The Jerusalem Bible, copyright © 1966 by Darton, Longman & Todd, Ltd. and Doubleday & Company, Inc. Used by permission of the publisher.

Those noted RSV are from the Revised Standard Version of the Bible, copyrighted 1946, 1952, © 1971, 1973 by the Division of Christian Education of the National Council of the Churches of Christ in the U.S.A. and are used by permission.

Those noted Barclay are from The New Testament: A New Translation, by William Barclay. © William Barclay 1968, 1969. Used by permission of Westminster Press.

Those noted NASV are from the New American Standard Bible © The Lockman Foundation, 1960, 1962, 1963, 1968, 1971, 1972, 1973, 1975, 1977. Used by permission.

Contents

Introduction

This book has been written as a deeply concerned response to the alarmingly influential rhetoric of Jerry Falwell, and others like him, in the militantly fundamentalist army of self-styled crusaders who consider themselves to be representative of that vaguely ominous creation of conservative "churchianity's" imagination, known more popularly as the Moral Majority. It has been said by some critics that the Moral Majority is neither, and to this I would quite agree. But it would be a dangerous blunder on the part of Mr. Falwell's opponents simply to dismiss as influentially impotent his attempts to control the morals of our country through the legislative mechanizations of the political process. "Church and State united" is the ultimate (even if unstated) goal on the fundamentalist agenda for "moral restoration." Their concerted efforts to defeat the ERA, their opposition to *any* abortion, and their tireless drive to eradicate the possibility of gay civil rights within our society—all demonstrate beyond the shadow of a doubt that these people have every intention of attempting to force upon the multireligious melting pot of American culture the narrowly rigid imperatives of fundamentalist Christian legalism.

As a member of the gay community, I feel particularly scandalized by those in the ranks of this religiously oriented political phenomenon who have galvanized themselves into an ethically offensive manifestation of misinformation, social prejudice, and antiintellectual biblical literalism. In relation to homosexuality, their moralistic campaign amounts to nothing less than an inflammatory vendetta against the integrity, personhood, and civil freedoms of all gay people. The implications of their continuing crusade against the gay community are only too apparent. With the ferocious zeal characteristic of misguided fanaticism, these homophobic Christians seem bent on a relentless holy war to deprive gay women and men of the basic rights afforded to all other citizens of this land.

Concerned Christians, both gay and non-gay, deplore, in the strongest terms, not only the tactics, but the bigoted beliefs concerning the "evils" of homosexuality with which the Moral Majority and others have sought to saturate the mass media. Their statements concerning the gay nature, life-style, and potential "threat" to the children of our society reveal virtually a total ignorance of these subjects. Almost every accusation made by Anita Bryant and her former organization (Save Our Children, Inc.) against homosexuals has been soundly contradicted by numerous experts in the fields of psychology, psychiatry, and criminology. Even their clouded and emotional theology is being repudiated by increasing numbers of thoughtful scholars throughout the nation. Obviously, Bryant and Falwell's credentials of infallibility in areas of disputed theological and sociological controversy have not been satisfactorily demonstrated to vast numbers of thinking and sensitive Christians.

Many of the accusations brought against gay people have been calculated to incite the ignorant, prejudiced, and misinformed, through a crusade that carries with it the spirit of the Salem witch-hunt, in a campaign that could easily erupt into fiery stakes of Inquisitional hate. Kill a Queer for Christ was the bumper sticker battle cry of many who supported Anita Bryant's drive against gays in Dade County, Florida, during 1977—a fitting commentary on the "Christian" virtues of that unfortunately successful crusade for fanaticism.

Sensitive Christians find the continual identification of such causes with the will of God to be a gross violation of the Third Commandment's basic spirit and intent; to use the name of the Lord as an instrument for oppressing others and denying certain people their human rights is truly to use God's name for blasphemous purposes. The attempt of the anti-gay fundamentalist lobby to take away from homosexuals the basic rights essential to human dignity, is, in fact, alienating thousands of gay people from any openness to the Good News of our Lord and Savior, precisely because homophobic Christians invoke God's name in such a cause. Mr. Falwell and his friends should take heed and beware, for their declarations to the effect that one cannot be a practicing Christian homosexual put them in the category of those religious hypocrites who were censured by Jesus for their bigoted and exclusionary legalism: "Woe to you . . . hypocrites, because you shut off the kingdom of heaven in front of people, for you do not enter in yourselves; nor do you allow those who are entering to go in" (Matthew 23:13).

Unfortunately, like some Pharisees of old, the Moral Majority and its associates seem to place greater value on the stony letter of the Law whose glory has faded (II Corinthians 3:7-11), rather than in the resplendent, eternal emanations of love and acceptance through Jesus Christ that the Spirit has made available to all people. Such blind fundamentalist legalism chooses to ignore the haunting specter of thousands of gay Christians who confess the same Lord and Savior as Jerry Falwell et al. These gay Christians are leading responsible, decent life-styles in their respective communities across the land, and they stand as an open rebuke to the homophobic generalization that all gay people are little more than "human rot." The capital that fearful evangelicals and fundamentalists have made of the fringe element in the gay community as being representative of the *whole* spectrum of homosexual society is no more fair or accurate than if they were to focus on pimps and prostitutes as being typical of the heterosexual life-style. Most saddening of all, however, is the continuing appeal to the holy Scriptures as a basis for coercing gays back into the closet of religious guilt. Through the use of isolated and misapplied biblical quotations, they have attempted to fan the flames of demonic prejudice and reactionism.

But there are many who see through the shallowness and pathetic parochialism of the Moral Majority with its multitudes of seemingly mindless minions, and they have begun to rise up in defiance of the prejudicial rhetoric and fear-mongering philosophy of Falwell's religious alliance. There are concerned gay and non-gay Christians who have every intention of being that proverbial thorn in the flesh, pricking the conscience of the church with regard to social tolerance and sexual understanding; and indeed, as our Lord said to Saul of Tarsus on the road to Damascus, "It is hard for you to kick against the thorns!"

There is a slogan that is often used in gay parades and demonstrations—Gay Is Good. And that is the theme of this book. However, certainly not *everything* popularized within the gay community as an acceptable or desirable life-style is constructively life-enhancing for the Christian homosexual; and it is this thorny issue that must be tackled in an objectively critical manner by those responsible for the leadership of the gay Community of Faith. Any response to the accusations of homophobic Christian propaganda must of necessity include a critical examination of the gay community itself, in those areas of ethical and moral vulnerability which seem to give credence to the assertions of anti-gay protagonists that homosexuals are sick, perverted, and immoral. Accordingly, the second part of this book will deal with the subject of gay sexual ethics, because it is imperative that our heterosexual opponents become aware of the fact that there are gay Christians who believe in responsible sexuality.

This book is not written as a timid, apologetic defense against the onslaught of homophobic condemnation. It is rather an aggressive attack upon those aspects of the Church of God which have sunk to the depths of reactionary discrimination and unthinking prejudice against our Lord's gay children. *Gays Under Grace* is not a polite presentation of soft-spoken appeals. It is a thunderous broadside, aimed at the very citadels of religious bigotry; and if even one stone can be dislodged from those walls, this book will have been a spiritual success.

Part One

GAY THEOLOGICAL PERSPECTIVES

Chapter 1

Let No One Take You to Task!

And although you were dead because of your sins and because you were morally uncircumcised, he has made you alive with Christ. For he has forgiven us all our sins; he has cancelled the bond which pledged us to the decrees of the law. It stood against us, but he has set it aside, nailing it to the cross. On that cross he discarded the cosmic powers and authorities like a garment; he made a public spectacle of them and led them as captives in his triumphal procession. Allow no one therefore to take you to task about what you eat or drink, or over the observance of festival, new moon, or sabbath. These are no more than a shadow of what was to come; the solid reality is Christ's.

Colossians 2:13-17 (NEB)

The early Christian community of Colossae, to which the apostle Paul addressed this message, faced a situation that is parallel in many ways to the dilemma of the contemporary gay Christian community. Those early believers were finding themselves pressured by the judgmental attitudes of persons outside the faith and, at the same time, were being condemned as second-class citizens of God's kingdom by the narrow-minded factions within the local church itself. The same problem exists for gay Christians today, but it is not without a solution.

For centuries, we of the gay community have been looked upon with contempt by the greater majority of society, in much the same way that the Gentiles were eyed with disdain by the Jewish nation, which called them dogs, and unclean. But in a vision to the

1

apostle Peter, God made it clear that with the coming of Christ to redeem all people, such an attitude could no longer be tolerated within the church (Acts 10:9-28). Similarly, the self-revelation of God is continuing in our day, declaring in that "still, small voice" to those who have a yielded conscience in the Body of Christ that prejudice based on sexual orientation is no less sinful and person-destroying than is discrimination based on race, sex, color, or creed.

Paul's advice to the Colossians is equally applicable to us to-day—"Allow no one to take you to task!" In the early church, the conflict over inclusion in the assembly of believers revolved around conformance to the social and ethical mores of the Jewish tradition. Following the same pattern, there are many modern pharisaical believers in the church who are seeking to impose on gay people an intolerable burden of guilt by insisting that we can-not truly walk with God in righteousness until we either renounce or suppress our sexual identity.

In the eyes of many conservative evangelical church leaders, an individual who continues to live the gay life-style while still claim-ing to be a Christian is obviously in a state of satanic deception and bound for hell. But we of the gay Community of Faith know better, for the apostle Paul declared, "Who are you to pass judg-ment on someone else's servant? Whether that person stands or falls is the business of the servant's Master, and that servant shall most certainly stand, because the Master has the power to enable that servant to stand" (Romans 14:4). As servants of the Lord, we realize that God is our only final and ultimate judge, and we feel certain that through the Holy Spirit's guidance and strength we shall eventually be vindicated. We will not allow other Christians to shake our faith by their homophobic tendencies toward reli-gious intimidation or by their gross misapplication of scriptural texts to reinforce their arguments. *Allow no one to take you to task!* This principle is being increasingly implemented by vigilant mem-bers of the gay Christian community through a forceful rejection of all such attacks against our stand as disciples of Jesus Christ. We cannot stop others from forming bigoted and derisive opinions based on their own intolerance, but we *can*, as informed, alert believers, refuse to be shaken or personally troubled by such pseudospiritual, fundamentalist propaganda.

In this struggle for justice within the Christian Church, gay people must of necessity begin to take the offensive by actively opposing all forms of homophobic bigotry being espoused by those church leaders who are following in the footsteps of the Moral Majority, just as Paul resisted Peter in the circumcision and foods issues (Galatians 2:11). It is a time for standing firm and attacking the narrow rigidness of biblical literalism being used by so many of our religious peers in the Body of Christ to justify their societal prejudices against gay people.

The issue of homosexuality in the church bears a striking resemblance to the first-century circumcision controversy with which Paul was so often confronted during his missionary journeys. His opponents insisted that in order to be a full partaker in the redemption and fellowship of Christ, a man must undergo the physical rite of circumcision and observe all the outward ordinances of the Jewish Law. Paul, however, refused to compromise his stand; he proclaimed that Jesus, through his life, death, and resurrection had fulfilled all the requirements of the Mosaic Law, which would have been impossible for human beings to accomplish (Romans 8:3-4). Through his redemptive mediation, Christ had brought the Law to an end, nailing it to his cross as a debt which had been paid in full by his precious blood (Romans 10:3-4; Colossians 2:14-15).

In this connection, there is a continuing thread of evidence which runs throughout the New Testament, demonstrating that the opponents of Paul's all-inclusive gospel were those whose primary concerns were the outward carnal regulations, inherently bound up in a legalistic system (Colossians 2:20-24). To these heretics, acceptance as a true believer was to be determined by one's attempt to fulfill the Law, with all its rites and observances. This teaching, in essence, denied the scope and sufficiency of the Atonement; it detracted from the glory due to Christ as the all-sufficient Mediator; and finally, it sought to impose on imperfect believers the impossible task of obeying an intricate Law, the spirit of which only Jesus in his unique spiritual maturity was able to perfectly exemplify through his complete dedication to the will of God. Time and again, we find Paul viciously attacking this circumcision heresy with a totally uncompromising stance, for it was a false doctrine that originated in the carnal human nature which thrives on a sense of *self*-sufficiency and *self*-righteousness in order to draw attention to supposed spiritual superiority. Paul warned the Galatian Christians of the underlying motives of these false teachers: "They [the circumcision advocates] eagerly seek you [for the purpose of being converted to their point of view], not commendably [for they condemned the Galatians' liberty in Christ], *but they wish to shut you out, in order that you may seek them*" (Galatians 4:17 NASV [emphasis mine]).

So also today, it is being made increasingly more obvious with the flood of anti-gay religious books and tracts, that the evangelical, fundamentalist, and charismatic branches of Christendom are fast becoming obsessed with a burning desire to see Christian gays come groveling back into the fold of their homophobic churches like the repentant prodigal son, complete with renunciations of their "sordid perversion." This is the evident hope of the religious homophobes, for in their socially prejudiced minds, it would be the ultimate demonstration of their own conception of themselves as the only real spokespeople for God, Country, and Transcendent Truth.

In actuality, fundamentalist believers are motivated to oppose the gay religious community more out of a subconscious sense of jealousy, for they simply cannot abide the thought that just *maybe* God is so loving, merciful, and magnanimous that he would use gay people as his instruments in the Body of Christ for a special purpose in reaching out to the outcasts of society whom the Lord has invited to the messianic banquet of his saving presence (Luke 14:16-24). Homophobic Christians no doubt shudder at the possibility that God could accept gay sexuality—something they have been socially programmed to abhor as the lowest of perversions. This generates much fear in the deep recesses of their hearts, for if such should be the case, then it stands to reason that possibly many of their supposed scriptural "certainties" will begin to evaporate like the morning dew. It will of necessity cause a painful reevaluation of certain theological assumptions they have come to utilize as security blankets to insulate them from the obligation of trying to find God's will anew in any given situation, rather than simply quoting a random sentence from the Bible (usually out of context) as being the established will of God in all times, situations, and circumstances. (There is only one real biblical principle that can be applied pervasively in any situation: "You shall love your neighbor as yourself"—a rule that evangelicals, fundamentalists, and charismatics are at present unable to do, for they still cannot find it within themselves to love us as whole, human, sexual beings made in the image of God—as gay people.)

In the truest sense of the term, the current alliance of evangelists, religious demagogues, and conservative churchianity is most definitely to be considered a modern revival of the "party of the circumcision." In Scripture, circumcision began with the Patriarch Abraham, who was, according to the Genesis account, commanded by God to perform the rite of surgically removing the foreskin of the penis of all the males in his household, as a sign of their covenant relationship with the Lord (Genesis 17:9-14). This ceremony was commanded as a perpetual statute throughout all the generations of Israel.

However, with the coming of Jesus as the long awaited Messiah, there came also the establishment of the New Covenant. Therefore the need for circumcision as a religious practice ceased, since it was the entrance rite for the former covenant, which now had been superceded. In the New Covenant, water baptism now became the sign of having been joined to the Community of God. Paul went to great lengths to explain the reasons for such changes in the Law (Romans 2:24-29; Colossians 2:11-13). Notwithstanding, there was still a sizable group of Jewish converts who were too entrenched in the commands and regulations of the Mosaic code to give them up. Not content with privately observing their traditions, they became convinced that it was necessary also for Gentile believers to keep the old Law, including circumcision.

It is illuminating to realize that this early church controversy was indirectly a *sexual* one, for circumcision was an operation performed on the sexual organ of the male child. Circumcision, therefore, is genitally related. So in essence, we find that under the Old Covenant Law, entering the fellowship of the Chosen People was dependant upon a quasi-sexual ritual which deprived a man's penis of its foreskin, foreshadowing the New Covenant's requirement that we forsake the lower nature of the flesh for the life-giving flow of the Spirit within. Paul argued that circumcision was now meaningless as a continuing religious observance, for if one violated the rest of the Law, then circumcision would avail one nothing in God's sight. He went on to sum up the matter quite succinctly: "For in Christ Jesus neither circumcision nor uncircumcision means anything, but faith working through love" (Galatians 5:6).

Not having learned this basic lesson, the prejudiced ecclesiastical accusers of the gay community are once again attempting to establish a new rite of circumcision as a prerequisite for the homosexual's salvation. This time, however, it is not a surgical knife that is being used to cut away the male foreskin; it is a jagged, psychic dagger of false teaching, whose double edges of guilt and condemnation seek to tear from gay people the wholeness of their natural sexual expression. But Paul's answer remains as a devastating put-down to the modern "circumcisers" of today when seen in perspective. All we need do is change two pivotal words in Galatians 5:6: For in Christ Jesus neither heterosexuality nor homosexuality mean anything, but faith working through love. The propaganda being espoused by numerous Christians—that a homosexual cannot be pleasing to God except through a "circumcision" of his or her natural sexual orientation—is an outright denial of the grace and acceptance that Jesus Christ has brought to "whosoever will." In the words of two courageously sensitive evangelical authors, "To tell homosexuals . . . that to enter God's kingdom they must cease to be homosexual, or at least cease expressing their homosexuality, is to place them under the law rather than under grace. Homosexuals cannot earn salvation by the sacrifice of their sexuality any more than heterosexuals can." [1]

It is most relevant to the issue if we notice that in the seventh chapter of his first Epistle to the Corinthian church, the apostle Paul formulated what could be called a principle of acceptance. When applied in the current context to Christians of the homosexual condition, it becomes a realistic and very Pauline way of handling the situation, much to the consternation of homophobic fundamentalists.

> Each one must order his life according to the gift the Lord has granted him *and his condition when God called him*. That is what I teach in all our congregations. Was a man called with the marks of circumcision upon him? Let him not remove them. Was he uncircumcised when he was called? Let him not be circumcised. Circumcision or uncircumcision is neither here nor there; what matters is to keep God's commands. *Every man should remain in the condition in which he was called.* Were you a slave when you were called? Do not let that trouble you; but if a chance of liberty

should come, take it. . . . *Thus each one, my friends, is to remain before God in the condition in which he received his call.*

I Corinthians 7:17-24 NEB (emphasis mine)

Of course, anti-gay opponents would immediately object to this application of the scriptural text. Their line of reasoning bases its premise upon the proposition that if this passage can be used to justify homosexuality as an acceptable "condition," then one could just as easily use it to condone other "conditions" such as adultery, murder, or prostitution. This argument is seriously defective, however, for Paul gave us two very concrete examples of conditions he considered to be rendered morally neutral because of their nature. He singled out the very pertinent examples of slavery and circumcision. Slavery was by no means a chosen condition. It was either inherited, by virtue of the fact that one was born into that social class, or it was imposed by circumstances beyond one's control. Similarly, circumcision was uniformly imposed on all Jewish male babies on the eighth day after their birth. Obviously there was little room for choice on the part of the children! On the other hand, adultery, murder, and prostitution are acts deliberately entered into, and therefore cannot be fairly compared to homosexuality. Nearly all experts agree that homosexuality is not chosen by the individuals who find themselves so predisposed. Professional investigation is confirming that our sexual orientation probably is determined either during pregnancy or in the very early years, prior to the age of five. It is also most appropriate to find that the great apostle wrote this gem of advice to the Corinthian Christians in the middle of a discourse dealing largely with questions of marriage, celibacy, and other sexually related matters, which makes the adaptation of this "acceptance principle" for the homosexually oriented most logical.

Just as in this passage of Scripture Paul makes the inconsequential nature of circumcision clear in its relation to our Christian walk, so also the application of this Pauline approach to the permanent sexual condition of gay people can be seen as both permissible and consistent. To rephrase the apostle: Homosexuality or heterosexuality is neither here nor there; what matters is to keep God's commands. It is not our sexual orientation that is foremost in God's concern, but the way we express that sexuality within the framework of God's commands for responsible, loving, sexual behavior.

NOTES

1. Letha Scanzoni and Virginia Ramey Mollenkott, *Is the Homosexual My Neighbor?: Another Christian View* (San Francisco: Harper & Row, 1978), p. 71.

Chapter 2
Religion's Reaction[1]

While we tend to view today's national press as a power-ful, essentially nonreligious conglomerate, smothering the country with its inexhaustible supply of news, stories, and opinions, few of us are sufficiently aware of the strong-ly influential religious press, which runs the gamut of theological variety—from the toxic disseminations of church sanctioned bigotry to the courageous convictions of insightful individuals who are shouting, with the silent voice of the printed page, a prophetic message to the stagnant institutional church. With the advent of Anita on the religious and political scene in early 1977, drumming up support for her battle against gay rights, various church periodi-cals were forced into the uncomfortable position of finding it neces-sary to take an open stand with regard to the whole homosexual issue, especially as it relates to ecclesiastical acceptance. True to form, most branches of the Christian church chose to "sit in the seat of the scornful" as the self-appointed Sanhedrin of the faith, nod-ding their heads in agreement with the female Caiaphas who was seeking the legal crucifixion of all homosexuals.

To be sure, there are a few thinking clerics within the confines of the established religious orders whose consciences have been touched by the Spirit; as a result, they are beginning to sense a deep concern for those segments of society that in the past have been designated as moral outcasts by the church. Yet for the most part, as the following excerpts will make abundantly clear, the church has continued its long-standing reputation for backward thinking and an inability to accept social change within the context of general Christian principles. A prime example is found in an editorial comment in the Foursquare World *Advance*, the official publication of the Foursquare Church.

> "I'm a Gay Christian!" brazenly boasted lapel pins sported by some supporters of a "Gay Rights" bill at a hearing conducted by an Oregon State Senate Committee considering such legislation. The Bible, however, thunders that such deviates are not Christians at all. . . .
>
> But nowadays a drive is underway to portray the practice [of homosexuality] as normal. It is never normal. Only if a pair of homosexual males produced a child through their abominable union—only if a pair of lesbians did likewise—could any pretense of normalcy be propagated.[2]

The ultimate logic of such reasoning can only force us to conclude that childless heterosexual marriages are not normal and, therefore, abominable. If the ability to procreate is to be considered the sole criterion for the normalcy of a sexual relationship, then homosexuals must surely not be alone in the Foursquare Church list of "abnormal minorities"!

Not to be outdone, *The Alliance Witness*, a magazine of the Christian and Missionary Alliance, also lapsed into editorial dementia by reeling in horror and disgust at the very thought of treating gay people as whole human beings with certain inalienable rights.[3] Farther on in the same article, gay people are referred to as having "twisted minds."

Common to both editorials is a consistent appeal to the Bible for magical proof texts, which, after being quoted, are never examined in their historical or cultural contexts. When making use, for example, of I Corinthians 6:9, the writers of both articles chose to demonstrate their poor scholarship by quoting from the Revised Standard Version, considered by many to contain the worst translation of this verse from the Greek in relation to the homosexual question. Interestingly enough, there were numerous cries from among the ranks of these and other conservative churches denouncing the RSV as a "communist conspiracy" and "the Devil's Bible" when it was first released by the National Council of the Churches of Christ. Yet now in desperation, they seem to be willing to use any source that may give the appearance of supporting their homophobic prejudices.

The most serious implication in both articles, however, was the assertion that gay people cannot be Christians. This statement borders perilously close to sinning against the Holy Spirit (Mark 3:29)—that is, attributing to Satan the works of the Holy Spirit in the lives of gay people who have confessed the name of Jesus as Savior. This is also an Antichrist message in a most insidious form, for it claims that because we are gay, Jesus Christ cannot be coming forth in us, permeating our lives through the ministry of the Holy Spirit. "Many deceivers have gone out into the world, those who do not acknowledge Jesus Christ as coming in the flesh. This is the deceiver and the antichrist" (II John 7). First-century Gnostics did not believe that Jesus had actually taken on a fleshly body through the Incarnation, for they considered matter and the flesh to be evil. In a similar manner, there are modern Gnostics (Gk.: *possessing knowledge* [know-it-alls?]) in the Christian Church who are denying that Christ can be regeneratively coming forth in us—in the flesh of gay persons—because they believe the practicing of our sexuality to be intrinsically evil. Therefore such a line of reasoning should be seen for what it is—a recent variation of an old Antichrist doctrine; and accordingly, it should be rejected as yet another form of self-righteous heresy.

In a slightly different vein, the Jesuit publication *America* could easily have been awarded a meritorious commendation for inconsistent journalism. In its June 25, 1977, edition, there appeared an editorial titled "Homosexuality and Civil Rights," which contains the important admission that:

> The use of biblical injunctions against homosexuality by Anita Bryant and her followers was hopelessly fundamentalistic. Theological scholarship, whether scriptural or ethical, recognizes today that the application of Scripture texts that condemn homosexuality is dubious at best. The phenomenon of homosexuality, as it is understood today, covers too wide a range of inclinations 'and behavior patterns to be subject to sweeping condemnations.

Yet in the same article is the denial that gays have any real need for protective civil rights:

> The argument in Dade County was not about the civil rights of individuals but about the social acceptability of certain

kinds of sexual behavior. ... The refusal by the voters to
accept an ordinance both unnecessary and in conflict with
community values was justified.[4]

What it did *not* say, however, is that such behavior has not been
considered socially acceptable in our culture precisely *because* of
the church and its misuse of the Bible to condemn homosexuality
as an abomination before God. From *America's* viewpoint, despite
almost two thousand years of oppression at the hands of ecclesiastical authority, which in turn has heavily influenced western
society against homosexuals, laws such as the defeated Miami
ordinance are still considered "unnecessary"!

Other churches are not so sure that homosexuality is to be
equated with sin. *The Presbyterian Survey* for June 1977 published
excerpts from a paper prepared by their Council on Theology and
Culture, which made the cautious observation that

in view of the complexity of the issue, the disagreement
among Christians and the variety in the character and experience of homosexual persons themselves, it seems un-
wise at this time to propose any one position as *the*
position of our Church.[5]

During this same time, a general synod of the United Church of
Christ went so far as to declare that the Anita Bryant crusade and
all it stood for was a portent of a new wave of reactionism which, if
not checked, could eventually undermine *everyone's* civil rights. It
also went on record as deploring the misuse of the Bible as an
instrument for instigation of group hatred and civil-rights violations against the gay community. Here, at least, is an indication
that there are a few rays of sunlight emerging from the cloudy
array of darkened religous homophobia.

One of the most surprisingly refreshing editorials was discovered tucked away on the last page of the July 6-13, 1977, issue of
Christian Century. Claiming to side with neither extreme in the
broiling gay rights controversy, famed historian, author, and professor Martin Marty still managed quite successfully to aim some
tongue-in-cheek pot shots at the Leviticus literalism of the Bryant
forces. By consistently adhering to the precepts of Leviticus,
Martin humorously concluded that only "conservative women
vegetarians" could pass the scrutiny of Old Testament legalism

unscathed. He then made the ingenious observation that I Corinthians 6:9-10 is just as embarrassing to Anita & Company as it is when applied against homosexuals:

> Finally, in Ms. Bryant's own favorite Bible verse, I Corinthians 6:10, homosexuals are told that they will not "inherit the kingdom of God." Nor will "the immoral, nor idolaters, nor adulterers ... nor drunkards ... nor robbers," all of whom make life easy in the conservative Orange Juice churches because, of course, there are none of such. But those dots also mark the omission of the word "revilers."
>
> Revilers won't inherit the kingdom. And while Anita often stuck to the text, her husband, Bob Green did some macho reviling of homosexuals. Out he goes. Now I'd better quit, stopping just short of reviling *him*. Otherwise the kingdom will have to get along without both Bob Green and me.[6]

Despite the ostrich philosophy of evangelical publications, hiding their heads in the sand of biblical literalism, not to mention the noncommittal approach of certain mainline denominational periodicals, there are nevertheless a few that, like voices crying in the wilderness, are proclaiming that every mountain of oppression must be flattened and every crooked path of prejudice be made straight. One such journal of Christian opinion is *Christianity and Crisis*. The combination May 30-June 13, 1977, issue was devoted entirely to the discussion of gay people in relation to the church. In the frontispiece, titled "The Debate on Homosexuality: We Vote for Change," the editors state that Christendom has entered its Valley of Decision and can no longer side-step the crucial problem of the homosexual condition.

> The difficulty for the churches is that to suspend judgment is no longer a possible course. When decisions are necessary, we have to presume that God's will can be discerned, if we have eyes to see, in the evidence at hand. In our reading of the evidence there is no longer a tenable case for excluding homosexuals from *full* participation in the life of the church and of society. ...
>
> As an independent religious journal *C & C* does not speak for the churches but to the churches. A journal of

opinion may risk its survival by voicing the wrong opinions, but a journal of opinion without opinions has no reason to survive. . . .

In determining human and ethical uses of sex, it is not the laws of biology we must consult but the law of love. To say this is not to relativize the scriptures or to make our burdens light; on the contrary, it is a hard saying. . . .

It is our view, however, that in the church the burden of proof rests on those who would maintain the policy of condemnation and ostracism that is our inheritance. And we believe that not the least consequence of a shift in this policy will be liberation and enlightenment for ourselves.[7]

Statements like this remind us that there is a prophetic remnant of believers in the Body of Christ who are calling upon the church to reexamine its conscience. Gay Christians are not alone. Although a minority in numbers, we can be a majority in God, for we can be conquerors in all things through Christ Jesus our Lord. Even as persecuted gay believers pass through the furnace of prejudicial hate and religious bigotry, One like unto the Son of God is walking in our midst. While the national religious press is busily engaged in the business of deciding upon the validity of our Christian experience as gay people, it is God in the court of heaven who shall bring judgment upon their judgment. The church has indeed been summoned to the valley of *God's* verdict, "for it is time for judgment to begin with the household of God" (I Peter 4:17), and whatever measure its people have used to condemn us, according to our Lord Jesus Christ, that same measure shall be used against them (Luke 6:38). Let those who so smugly consign gays to the consuming anger of God's wrath take heed, lest when they stand before the judgment seat of Christ the pronouncement come upon them: "You have been weighed on the scales and found deficient" (Daniel 5:27).

NOTES

1. A version of this chapter appeared in the August 1977 issue of *In Unity*, the official magazine of the Universal Fellowship of Metropolitan Community Churches, under the title "Religious Press in the Valley of Decision."
2. Raymond Cox, "Current Events & Comments," Foursquare World *Advance* (June 1977), p. 15.

3. H. Robert Cowles, "Editorial Voice—Gay: The Bible Calls It Sin," *The Alliance Witness* (June 15, 1977), p. 31. (The author of this editorial preferred not to be directly quoted in this book [?]).

4. "Homosexuality and Civil Rights," *America*, editorial (June 25, 1977). Reprinted with permission of America Press, Inc., 106 West 56th Street, New York, N.Y. 10019. © All Rights Reserved.

5. Quoted from the *Minutes* of the 117th General Assembly of the Presbyterian Church in the United States, p. 338, li. 929-33.

6. Martin E. Marty, "M.E.M.O.: Speaking Literally," Copyright 1977 Christian Century Foundation. Reprinted by permission from the July 6-13, 1977, issue of *The Christian Century*.

7. Robert G. Hoyt, "We Vote for Change," *Christianity and Crisis* (May 30-June 13, 1977). © Christianity and Crisis, Inc. Reprinted by permission.

Chapter 3

The Homophobic Book-Binge

During the past decade, with the increasing candidness in relation to sexual subjects once considered taboo, there has been a steady increase of books, usually in a favorable vein, on topics such as homosexuality. In retaliation, there has been a corresponding upsurge in the publication of Christian books, producing a literal book-binge that has glutted the religious literary market in an attempt to describe the dangers of "shameless homosexual degradation." In the following pages, we will be examining a sort of eclectic collage of high points in fundamentalist absurdity and shortsightedness, extracted from representative examples found in the current flood of printed religious homophobia. We can by no means make reference to all the books that have been disseminated through the publishing houses of conservative Christianity in its relentless attack upon gay people and their moral integrity. That is not the purpose of this particular investigation. However, with selected examples, it will be decisively demonstrated that there are major flaws in the reasoning of typical evangelical anti-gay rhetoric, as well as misapplication and misunderstanding of crucial biblical texts.

One of the earliest homophobic polemics to have any widespread distribution was a chapter found in *The Untapped Generation*, authored by David and Don Wilkerson, of Teen Challenge fame. Containing thinly veiled contempt sprinkled generously with sanctimoniously slanderous statements, this book clearly reveals a lack of spiritual as well as psychological perception.

17

The homosexual practices his sin because he chooses and professes his own wisdom, contrary to God's. He has substituted futile thinking for truth and reality. . . .

Overt homosexuality can be traced to serving the flesh, rather than God. When a person no longer honors and serves God, he is susceptible to becoming a slave of the flesh. Before one can become a life-time homosexual, he must ignore the voice of conscience, his knowledge of right and wrong, and follow a premeditated course of disobedience and stubbornness.[1]

Some of the authors' statements are almost sadly ludicrous. The accusation that gays "choose" their sexual orientation as "a premeditated course of disobedience and stubbornness" is flatly contradicted by the observation of most psychologists and researchers that "the impulses of both homosexuality and heterosexuality seem to develop quite unconsciously and that we emerge as one or the other, or some combination of both, quite apart from any conscious act of will or desire." [2] In relation to the counseling of a young boy about his homosexual feelings, another author comments,

The one point of general agreement seems to be that our sexual tendencies have been developed, basically, by at least the age of puberty.... The one honest, helpful response we can give this boy is to let him realize that, as far as we now know, he didn't consciously bring about, out of his own desire and will, the sexual feelings he now has.[3]

It seems that the Wilkersons are trying to create a caricature of demonic rebelliousness, as if all gay people were bent on thwarting God's purpose for their lives. Such insinuations and/or accusations amount to slander against many Christian gays. Bearing false witness against one's neighbor is not exactly a virtue to be exemplified by a Christian minister or writer!

The Wilkersons' overgeneralization reaches idiotic proportions when they claim that

a homosexual is a victim of a mind and imagination given over to the worship of the flesh. The homosexual feeds on filthy literature, on dirty pictures and lewd novels. His dreams, thoughts and imagination have been taken over by the demons of lust.[4]

All one need do is substitute *heterosexual* in the above excerpt to observe just how distorted a product of personal prejudice such a comment really is. The description does not apply to homosexuals in general, and especially not to gay Christians, any more than it applies to all heterosexuals. Furthermore, the authors have put themselves in the indefensible position of equating sexual desire with "worship of the flesh." If such be the case, then *all* sex is hopelessly idolatrous and sinful. They conveniently forget that sexual desire, whether heterosexual or homosexual, is the same natural urge, with only the object of that desire differing, depending on one's sexual orientation.

As a last pitiable resort, the Wilkersons list "demon possession" as a contributing cause of the gay person's sexual impulses. This is a recurring phenomenon of fundamentalist logic: What one does not understand or cannot adequately explain must be blamed upon demons! Shades of Salem and its puritanical madness still seem to be a significant influence upon Christian literalists—one of the many shadowy skeletons rattling in the closet of the conservative evangelical mentality. Upon reflection, one wonders whether the Wilkersons are of such a mind-set as to sincerely believe that the homosexual Michelangelo was "taken over by demons of lust" while he painted the nude creation scenes upon the ceiling of the Sistine Chapel? (It is amusing to note that a "demon-awareness" revival has recently taken a firm hold in fundamentalist circles. One book by a pair of self-declared "deliverance" ministers has actually gone so far as to state that not only is homosexuality caused by demons, but that we should avoid purchasing stuffed toy frogs or anything in the image of an owl, because demons love to inhabit them)![5]

Gini Andrews, another evangelical writer, in her book *Sons of Freedom* has even treated homosexuality and bisexuality in the same category with child rape, kleptomania, sadomasochism and nymphomania.[6] She seems to be uninformed of the fact that both homosexuality and bisexuality are sexual orientations, whereas the other conditions are forms of either sexual or psychological disorder. The American Psychiatric Association has officially removed homosexuality from its list of mental maladies.

While chastising most of the psychological and psychiatric profession for its reticence to claim a cure for homosexuals, Andrews, in seeming desperation, appeals for support to the studies of psychoanalyst Irving Bieber, who claimed to have "cured" a significant percentage of his homosexual patients. However, the conclusions of Bieber's study fall far short of establishing scientific fact.

> Bieber's book (1962) is a strange mixture of astute clinical observations and the worst kind of pseudo science.... Bieber starts out with the assumption that homosexuality is a mental illness and finds, perhaps not surprisingly, that his clinical findings support his assumption!... Subjecting the responses of Bieber's colleagues to statistical analysis does not obviate the fact that these responses derive from a clinical procedure (psychoanalysis) which yields results which are still to a large extent speculative, and which represent primarily the original, very insightful, theoretical assumptions of the early analysts....
>
> The flaws in Bieber's method are twofold: First, any inquiry that seeks to use only one kind of data to the exclusion of other data in order to substantiate a preconceived conclusion is not scientific; second, such data which do seem to support the preconceived conclusion may also be used, and perhaps even more advantageously, to support many other conclusions which the investigator has rejected on no other grounds than his prejudice.[7]

Needless to say, it will take a lot more evidence than that of Irving Bieber to establish the "sickness" of gay people. Grave suspicions also have been cast upon Bieber's claims by other authorities in the field of behavioral studies. In referring to Bieber, C. A. Tripp describes a most interesting story that most homophobic Christian authors are eager to avoid in their presentation of the "facts."

> After Kinsey's death, *and to this day*, Wardell Pomeroy (a longtime member of the Research and now a New York psychotherapist) has maintained a standing offer to administer the Kinsey Research battery to any person a therapist might send, and thus possibly validate a case of changed homosexuality. *This offer has never had any "takers" except for one remarkable instance.*
>
> A New York psychiatrist [Bieber] ... who has written an important book on the subject in which various percentages of changed cases were reported—did indeed make a definite commitment to exemplify these results. After sever-

al delays of several weeks each, the psychiatrist finally confessed to Pomeroy *that he had only one case which he
thought would qualify* but that, unfortunately, he was on
such bad terms with the patient he did not feel free to call
him up. One possible case?—then what about his 358-page
book claiming from 19 to 50 per cent cures? ... Over the
years there have been literally dozens of second-party
accounts of "cured" homosexuality. *Like the footprints of
the Loch Ness monster, they very often appear, but without
the presence of the elusive beast.* (emphasis mine) [8]

Still another book, *On Lonely Street with God* by Duane Pederson, attempts to capitalize on the loneliness and guilt of many
homosexuals in its appeal for them to accept Christ and be
"changed." [9] But as one counseling guidance graduate has
pointed out, the cause of loneliness and associated guilt feelings is
not the homosexual orientation itself, but rather the pressure of
society's (including the church's) attitude toward it.

> If the homosexual client says that he wants to change to
> heterosexuality because he's unhappy in "gay" life, I want
> to explore with him what is making him unhappy. Many
> times I have found that the basis of this unhappiness
> comes from the social attitudes that this country has
> towards homosexuality. Like any other minority group
> attempting to survive in a hostile and bigoted environment,
> they too succumb to unrelenting prejudice with reactions
> of self-doubt, self-blame, and self-hate. Many homosexuals
> have "bought" the myth of their own inferiority, and sadly
> have cooperated in their own destruction. This is under-
> standable when every voice, including parents and siblings,
> condemns and derides. I feel that therapy for the homosex-
> ual at some point must help him to love himself and take
> pride in the experiment of living that he has undertaken.[10]

Most anti-gay evangelicals utilize the standard timeworn
guesses for the causes of homosexuality—a weak father image, fear
of women, and so on—none of which have proved either adequate
or reliable as an overall explanation of what is known to some as
the gay phenomenon. A prime example of such root-cause stereo-
typing is found in one charismatic pamphlet dealing with
homosexuality:

One of the root problems of the homosexual is often a life source that was tragically deficient in true authority. A domineering, pushy mother and a receding passive father—or in some cases a seemingly opposite pattern in an over-protective, coddling mother and a harsh hyper-critical father—will confuse the divine authority which was established in the home. The loss of the authority [of the father as head of the household] will not only produce sexual role identity problems, but leave a child spiritually uncovered and vulnerable to malicious attack [from demons?].[11]

It is truly unfortunate that so many Christian writers who attempt to do scholarly research on this subject choose only to scratch the surface of the various psychological studies dealing with homosexual origins. This is most probably due to their over-confident attitude—that their interpretation of the relevant scriptural data is the only right approach to the ultimate truth—which in turn results in demeaning the behavioral-science studies that contradict their assumptions. The truth notwithstanding, homophobic Christians tend to select only those psychiatric theories that seem to support their legalistic biblical beliefs, most of which are archaic or have been refuted by more recent studies. The above quotation is a perfect example. An uninformed layperson who reads such dogmatic assertions would be led, by the very air of authority with which the author of the pamphlet writes, to assume that the "dominant mother" theory must be an unchallenged and readily provable fact. Such, however, is not true. In C. A. Tripp's monumental work *The Homosexual Matrix*, he explores this generally accepted misconception:

It is still widely believed that homosexuality stems from "identity problems." . . . By far the chief villain in the play is the dominant, the smothering, or the close-binding mother. (The dominant-mother theory has come into such extraordinary prominence as to deserve a special note. For good reasons, *sex researchers have never accepted the notion, but it has had quite a run in both armchair psychiatry and low-grade popular sociology*—perhaps helped along in recent years by the fashionable tendency to attribute any individual's plight less to factors within himself than to some outside authoritarian oppressor. The dominant mother seemed to fit the shoe. [After cataloguing a list of maladies blamed upon the dominant mother by early theories, including alcoholism, schizophrenia, and drug addiction, Tripp concludes:] Thus, the whole issue has become ridiculous on its surface; underneath, it is a technical monstrosity. *Certainly the mother-son closeness that sometimes occurs in homosexuality is far better interpreted as the PRODUCT than as the cause of the disposition which supports it.*) (emphasis mine).[12]

Ironically enough, the Jehovah's Witnesses, in their publication *Awake!* proved the weakness of these worn-out arguments while they were attempting to illustrate the sinfulness and futility of the gay life-style. They keenly observed that lack of strong fatherly leadership in a household has never been proved to have such a uniform effect on young boys that it would predispose them toward homosexual tendencies. The fact that many boys have grown up without a father and have not emerged as homosexuals is indicative of the inherent weakness of the "close, binding mother/ weak, passive father" theory as an adequate explanation of gay origins. *Awake!* then made an important confession that most evangelicals and fundamentalists would do well to ponder: One precise cause of homosexuality that would be accurately applicable to all gay people has not yet, with any final degree of certainty, been discovered.[13] As food for thought, perhaps we should also ask the experts whether the exact cause of heterosexuality has been discovered?

Another more recent book, Tim LaHaye's *The Unhappy Gays*, is enjoying a wide range of popularity among Christians who generally have little knowledge of or exposure to homosexual people. An adequate critique of his work would necessitate more space and verbiage than it is worth. However, a few of his classic insanities will suffice. Among the more bizarre conclusions reached by LaHaye is his belief that the coming Antichrist will probably be a homosexual! This he attempts to suggest by reference to Daniel 11:37.

As we approach the end of the age and the return of Christ, we can expect that homosexuality, among other degenerating sin practices, will increase. In fact, Daniel 11:37 contains an interesting prediction about the anti-Christ, who is destined to rule the world just prior to our Lord's return to set up his Kingdom. "Neither shall he regard the God of his fathers, *nor the desire of women. . . ."* This suggests that the anti-Christ *may* be a homosexual. If he is, that would explain the significance of the influential group of international homosexuals who are rumored to be gaining worldwide political influence.[14]

Of course, such an insinuation is calculated to strike terror into the hearts of good fundamentalist believers, for nothing could be more evil than society's assimilation of the very attributes of the Antichrist! However, upon closer examination, it is plain that LaHaye failed to do his homework while researching the supposedly forthcoming Man of Sin's possible sexuality. A casual referral to some recent and more accurate translations totally knocks the props out from under his flimsy theory. The following translation of Daniel 11:37 is taken from The New English Bible: "He will ignore his ancestral gods, *and the god beloved of women;* to no god will he pay heed but will exalt himself above them all" (emphasis mine). The "desire of women" quoted by LaHaye from the King James Version has nothing whatsoever to do with sexual orientation, but is a description of the popular god Adonis-Tammuz, whose cult had numerous women devotees. This is confirmed by a footnote in the commentary of The Jerusalem Bible.[15]

If we take the typical futuristic scheme of prophetic interpretation adapted by most evangelicals as correct, then the most we can legitimately infer is that the main message of the prophet Daniel in this passage is a warning that the coming satanic world ruler will not respect the prevailing religious traditions of his time, but exalt himself above all religions as the very god incarnate. In fact, there are many New Testament scholars who feel that the apostle Paul was reiterating this theme in II Thessalonians 2:1-8. In regard to LaHaye's supposed inside scoop on some international homosexual political conspiracy, let the readers judge for themselves in light of his paranoid homophobia!

LaHaye further parades his poor scholarship for all to see:

> In 2 Timothy 3 we find a list delineating nineteen characteristics of the "last days." People are to be "without natural affection." . . . "Without natural affection" refers to sexual perversion: homosexuality.[16]

Most translators would not agree with this dogmatic assertion, as we can see from the translation of these words in more modern renditions:

"without love"................New International Version
"unloving" ....New American Standard Version
"heartless" ....The Jerusalem Bible

Paul was simply repeating Jesus' earlier warning—that at the end of the age, "because of the increase of wickedness, the love of most will grow cold" (Matthew 24:12 NIV). The verse in question obviously does not refer to homosexuality. In light of such weak arguments and unresearched assumptions, it would be fair to conclude that astute scholarship does not seem to be one of LaHaye's strong points. On this basis alone, it is quite reasonable to call into question the validity of his many other authoritarian-sounding claims and derogations.

Evangelical Presbyterian writer Don Williams has also penned a very influential book attacking the acceptance of homosexuality by the church. In *The Bond That Breaks*, he too has come up with some puzzling, if not logic-defying statements.

The New Testament rules out adultery, fornication and homosexual acts as proper expressions of sexuality. All violate God's intention that male and female be "one flesh." None display the relationship of Christ and the church. . . . We are not fulfilled simply in "loving relationships" without regard to their structure. If this were the only standard, what ground would there be for excluding loving, fulfilling incest or bestiality?[17]

Williams, along with many other evangelicals, makes certain assumptions, which in turn can lead to some most outlandish conclusions. In the first place, while both adultery and fornication are definitely ruled out as proper expressions of sexuality, this ban cannot be extended to *all* homosexual activity, in light of the most accurate and thorough treatment of scriptural content and exegesis, when examined with our knowledge of modern psychological insights into the nature of sexual inversion.

It is also interesting to note that Williams seems to have a basic misunderstanding in his application of the "one flesh" principle.

Adultery, fornication, and homosexual acts, he says, all violate the intention that man and woman should be one flesh, implying that only in heterosexual marriage can two persons properly become "one flesh." Paul, on the other hand, approached the subject of sexual immorality from a totally opposite premise. It was precisely *because* those who indulged in prostitution and irresponsible sexuality were technically becoming one flesh through their illicit activities that he condemned such behavior (I Corinthians 6:15-20). For Paul, the issue was not that such immorality precluded the possibility of becoming one flesh, but rather that prostitutional fornication took the concept of one flesh/one body out of the context of humanizing, loving, committed relationship; therefore denying the will of God and Christ's sovereignty in guiding and expressing our relationships. In I Corinthians, I believe it is evident that Paul regarded all forms of sexual union as means of becoming one flesh. However, in the mind of the great apostle, the moral acceptability of such unions was determined by whether or not they glorified Christ and fulfilled the highest intentions of love-in-relationship. Obviously, fornication and adultery do not. But with regard to homosexual acts, it can safely be said that the "one flesh" principle is just as applicable. Sexual union, whether heterosexual or homosexual, produces a physical, sensual, emotional, and very often a psychic bonding between two persons that, depending upon the context, can be either destructive and degrading, or highly constructive as a means of relational interpenetration in the bonds of love.

Williams is also heavily influenced by the symbolic analogies in the Bible, especially that in Ephesians 5:31-32, in which the relationship between Christ and the church is compared to that between husband and wife. From this Williams concludes that only a heterosexual relationship can "mirror the relationship between Christ and the church." [18] By imposing such limitations, he is implying that in some mysterious way these scriptural analogies of marriage must be *more* than mere symbolism—must suggest a sexual reality in regard to the interaction between the Lord and his church. This, of course, Williams would deny, but the simple fact remains that if only a *hetero*sexual relationship can demonstrate the love of Jesus for his church, then it must be an indication that Christ's affections for the church are rooted to some extent in feelings of human heterosexuality! As said before, bizarre conclusions from this line of reasoning are not hard to come by!

However, if one wishes to pursue this overly literalistic approach to biblical metaphors, one may be quite shockingly enlightened. In the writings of Paul, the church is variously described as a bride and as a virgin (Ephesians 5:27; II Corinthians 11:2). But that "bride" is made up of both male and female constituents (Galatians 3:28), implying either an inherent bisexuality, or else a hermaphroditic nature within the bride! Furthermore, in chapter 4:13, this same Epistle to the Ephesians makes reference to the Church as being "a mature male" [Gk.]. We know from the Gospels that Jesus is a glorified male human being. What then, is the real gender of the bride? Female? Male? Or both? Is the bride really a hermaphrodite? This is not meant to be blasphemous, but to point home to the reader the dangers of creating reality from the symbolic. To continue in this vein, it would be easy enough to justify heterosexuality, because in relation to Christ, the church is called the bride; homosexuality, because in relation to Christ, the church is called a mature male; and last but not least, autoeroticism, because the church is described as being Christ's own body!

Finally, Williams complains that we cannot give moral credence to homosexual relationships simply because they may be very loving and tender. This, he says, would logically lead to a condoning of incest and bestiality on the same grounds. There are serious flaws in this argument, too. What we would consider incest (Leviticus 18) was frequently practiced in the earliest times. The early Genesis accounts testify to this in such examples as Cain, who, if he were to have a wife at all, would have had to marry his sister (Genesis 4:17). It is interesting to note that incestuous relationships are condemned time and again in the Holiness Code, because such close relatives "are your own flesh: it would be incest" (Leviticus 18:17 JB). Ironically, on the basis of this criteria, the most incestuous relationship of all time was that of Adam and Eve, for in Adam's own words, Eve was "bone from my bones, and flesh from my flesh" (Genesis 2:23 JB)! Actually, the later prohibition against incest, which was carried over into the New Testament (I Corinthians 5:1-5), stemmed from the need to protect humanity from the debilitating effects of physical and mental degeneration that often resulted from continual intermarriage. This was not the case immediately after the Creation, for humans lived longer, were stronger and, generally speaking, had not yet been negatively affected by the Fall.

At this time, incest has been either discouraged or forbidden, due to its effects upon the offspring of such relationships. Hence its suppression has been founded upon a loving consideration for the unborn. In fact, incestuous liaisons have been prohibited precisely *because* of their *heterosexual* nature, complete with disastrous reproductive possibilities. Therefore, for Williams to classify homosexuality with incest is not only misleading, but illogical. The reasons for banning incest are inherent in its heterosexual nature. Homosexuality cannot be compared or condemned with incest. Their unrelatedness could not be more striking.

Williams also classifies gay sexuality on a level with bestiality, and he is not alone in this among homophobic writers. But such a comparison is again unwarranted, for homosexual relations do not transgress the natural order as do the practices of bestiality. The seriousness of that sin lies in its transgression of order: God's command was for the beasts of the earth to reproduce "after their own kind" (Genesis 1:24). Any attempt to relate sexually with animals indicates perversion of one's common humanity, a desire to descend to the level of the beast. Homosexuality cannot be compared in this instance, either, since gays do not seek to transgress the order of their own humankind.

There is probably no greater or better known evangelist, with the exception of Billy Graham, than the controversial faith healer Oral Roberts. In his popular book *How to Get Through Your Struggles*, he makes some of the most sweeping, shallow, and professionally naive assertions imaginable about the nature and "cure" of homosexuality. In a conversation he once had with a distraught mother who had discovered that her son was a homosexual, Roberts had sought to comfort and encourage her by positively affirming the following points:

1. Her son could change and put aside his homosexuality.
2. The evangelist had personally witnessed the transformation of *many* homosexuals.
3. A change from homosexual to heterosexual was usually accomplished in a rapid fashion over a short period of time, after conversion to Christ.
4. The Creation account in Genesis 1 rules out the legitimacy of homosexuality, by virtue of the fact that people were created male and female.

5. Homosexual tendencies are not congenital or hereditary, but rather the result of moral weakness.[19]

Several of Roberts' points should be critically examined, to show conclusively just how deceptive such "authoritative" statements can be for unwitting readers of such literature—readers who generally have no informed awareness of homosexuality and its complexity. Roberts' declaration that he has personally witnessed the "miracle of change" in *many* homosexuals is tantamount to a statement of "theotherapeutic" success unequaled in the field of psychiatry, psychology, or any other area of behavioral treatment.[20] But when the chips are down, and concrete substantiation is demanded, it is fairly certain that Roberts' claim of having witnessed numerous cases of complete sexual reorientation would be laughed off the witness stand in any hypothetical court of law. His testimony that homosexuals have been "changed" and "healed" is just another rubber-stamp apologetic in the recently established tradition of evangelical wishful thinking regarding gay "deliverance." Roberts is only one of a growing number of fundamentalists who are peddling the pretentious claims of the ex-gay gospel. But according to psychotherapist Ralph Blair, director of the Homosexual Community Counseling Center in New York City and the guiding light of Evangelicals Concerned (one of the very few evangelical organizations advocating acceptance and understanding of homosexuals within the church), those reports of gay "deliverance" and "change" are actually little more than the proverbial chaff in the wind:

> Some people now are making claims that there are those who have been changed from homosexual orientation to heterosexual through Christian conversion, prayer, exorcism, Spirit-baptism, or divine healing. Nonetheless, I have found that such truly reversed people are as rare a breed as are those supposedly changed through therapy. Put as simply as possible: there is no validated evidence that they exist.
>
> Even though the popular Christian press has often been as naive as was the earlier popular secular press in reporting such "miracle cures" without doing some sound inves-

tigative reporting, there can be found no validated case of sexual reorientation through any spiritual means. . . . What has been found, not only involves fraud but self-deception, diagnostic error and confusion, placebo effects, psychopathological denial, disillusionment, and even eventual suicide.[21]

Another objection raised by evangelist Roberts is the ill-thought-out contention that since humans were created male *and* female, it is therefore incumbent that *all* sexual expression be limited to relations with the opposite sex. After all, it is reasoned, since God told Adam and Eve to be fruitful and multiply, heterosexual expression is clearly the only form of sexual union ever sanctioned by God; and it is, therefore, what God intended to be "normal" for the behavior of the human race. However, Roberts and others fail to take into consideration that, while accepting heterosexual activity as "the norm," it is possible that divergences from this norm could be an aspect of preconceived variations planned by the Creator, adding yet another intricate piece to the beauty and variety of the divine design for life's expression.

Furthermore, if such universal and timeless applicability is to be attributed to God's command to the first human parents, then our fundamentalist opponents, if they are to be consistent, must preach just as vehemently against any form of birth control, since God's declared primary intent at that time was for them to multiply (Genesis 1:28). From this we could just as logically argue that people who marry without the intention of having children are out of the will of God, and as a consequence, their sexual activity together can only be viewed as unnatural and an intentional thwarting of God's revealed will.

There is also another danger that arises in the tendency to overemphasize the male-and-female-togetherness theme of the first chapter of Genesis: Such emphasis implies a certain lack of completion in God's purpose when individuals choose to remain single. From Genesis 2:24, in which it is stated that a man shall leave father and mother to cleave unto a wife, it could be argued, by stretching the point, that no man should be without a wife. Hence it would be logical to conclude that singleness must be a sin, since it is not in line with the Lord's original intent at the time of creation.

Of course, we can see how specious this kind of logic really is in the light of common sense and balanced realism (a rare commodity among many conservative evangelicals). These false deductions to which overly literalistic biblicism can lead us are yet further examples of the extremes of a mind satiated with one-dimensional scripturalism. It places an overemphasis on the biblical words, with no corresponding appreciation for their larger historical and mythic contexts.[22]

For all Oral Roberts' attempts to present himself and his ministry as a modern, sophisticated medium for Christian healing and compassionate counsel, he has not been able to conceal the intellectual deficiency inherent in his thinking on homosexuality, as well as on other socially relevant issues—a mind-set that predictably has been warped by his bondage to biblical literalism. So we can see that the tired, harping objection continually raised by Roberts and others, to the effect that if God had wanted homosexuals, he would have created Adam and Bruce or Eve and Vivian, is similar to insisting that if God had wanted humans to fly, he would have given them wings! Actually, flying in airplanes is a more "unnatural" practice for humans than same-sex activity, since at least the evidence of natural, primate behavioral patterns testifies to the existence of homosexuality as a prevalent deviation from the general norm of heterosexuality. On the other hand, attempts of the human race to ascend into the heavens seem to be rooted in a desire to transcend the limits of our created environment by unnatural and artificial means. So we see that homophobic logic cannot have it both ways. If it were necessary for everything acceptable as a median for human behavior to have been present in Eden and mentioned as such in Scripture in order to be permissible for the Christian and therefore "natural," we quickly perceive that the limitations of that which constitutes the "natural" would be severe indeed!

It should not be forgotten that there are other "ex-gay" ministries which, like that of Oral Roberts, have sought to buttress their arguments by a strong appeal to "the Creator's original intent" in making humans male and female. Some even go so far as to insist that the image of God cannot be fully expressed or reflected in human beings apart from heterosexual union.[23] This school of thought contends that the image and likeness of God, made reference to in Genesis 1:26, is actually the human male and female gender identities described in verse 27. Seen in this light, male and female identities were not created into the fabric of human ana-tomical composition simply to insure the procreative process and survival of the race, but rather for the primary purpose of imaging the Deity's likeness as a male/female God. According to this reasoning, then, homosexual union cannot mirror the image of God-in-relationship and is therefore a flagrant thwarting of the Creator's original intent.

What is absolutely amazing to me is the incredible philo-sophical shortsightedness into which some Christians are led by homophobic desperation, manifested by their continual attempts to prove too much from isolated chapters and texts of Scripture. The rationale of the last argument fails on at least three counts. First, by insisting that maleness and femaleness are part of God's image, they have anthropomorphized the Deity with gender identity, which necessitates humanlike form and substance. Only the strange labyrinth of Mormonism (with its belief that God the Father is simply a glorified human being) could embrace such an idea. Certainly traditional Christian interpretation has always held to the reported affirmation of Christ that "God is Spirit" (John 4:24)—not some genderized, anthropomorphic deity reminiscent of pagan Greek mythology. Second, by ascribing male and female identity to the nature of God, they have sexualized God in much the same way the ancient Middle Eastern fertility cults once did. To state that the only way God's image can be fully reflected is in the sexual union of male and female is to state the foundation for pagan fertility religion. In fact, part of the basis for ceremonial temple prostitution was the hope that through sexual intercourse with the sacred prostitutes, there would be "imaging," as it were, (and encouraging) of the sexual activity of gods and goddesses, which in turn would secure the fertility of the land.

If God's image can be fully realized only in heterosexual union, then Jesus, as a presumably single person, could not have fully mirrored the likeness of the invisible God—something Paul emphatically says that he *did* do in his capacity as the Second Adam, the Son of humankind (Mark 13:26; I Corinthians 15:45; Colossians 1:15). This idea also implies that human beings who live as single individuals do not and cannot fully reflect the divine image.

Furthermore, applying even more questioning logic to this

dilemma, we find that if God is viewed from the Judaic concept of essential Oneness and singular Unity of Being, then the above-mentioned theory would transform the Deity into a hermaphrodite! Similarly, when viewed through the lenses of traditional trinitarian orthodoxy, one would no doubt be led to inquire whether the Persons of the Trinity carry on a sexual interrelationship within the Godhead! And to further complicate such theological insanity, if both Father and the Son are viewed as "male," the Holy Spirit must therefore be "female," if the male/female nature of the Godhead is to be in any way demonstrable. Does the Father have heterosexual union with the Holy Spirit, or does the Son? Or do both? Is sexual interaction within the Trinity therefore incestuous in nature? The logical progression of questions that arise as a result of ascribing sexual gender to God's Being is the most potent indication of its absurdity.

Third, one of the more subtle flaws of this argument is its evident confusion of maleness/femaleness with those perceived attributes of divinity which often reflect God's nature in terms of masculine and feminine interaction. Maleness and femaleness are limited solely to sexual gender identity. On the other hand, masculinity and femininity are patterns of behavior and self-expression and are not restricted to the physiological limitations of respective gender differences. There are, for example, women who reflect, psychologically and behaviorally, primarily "masculine" traits, while there are men who are predominantly "feminine" in orientation. This fact alone enables us to arrive at a most logical deduction: If masculinity and femininity are viewed as attributes that are constituent aspects of God's image, then such "imaging" of God on the part of human beings cannot be limited to heterosexual expression. In many homosexual relationships, one partner often displays a more masculine demeanor, in contrast to his or her partner's more recessive and passive feminine characteristics. Even more important, each individual is a complex and fluctuating combination of both masculine and feminine tendencies, as Carl Jung so strikingly demonstrated with his psychological conceptualization of the "anima" and the "animus" resident respectively in all men and women.

When we take all this into consideration, we are led to the inescapable conclusion that to complement masculine with feminine does not require heterosexual intercourse. Indeed, such blending interaction between the two extremes is admirably displayed in the unique psychological and emotional makeup of each individual. In actuality, the homophobic "gender union = divine image" theory almost totally ignores the traditional understanding of the Imago Dei as being *interior*, corresponding to the Spirit within, which enables the human being to stand apart from the rest of creation in a God-like capacity for reason, conscience, and creativity. It has nothing to do with an *external* image related to the sexual union of opposite genders.

But we are not finished with our inspection of Oral Roberts, for his miracle claims and overstated assumptions have not yet been exhausted. One of his most incredulous statements was that usually, when a homosexual becomes a Christian, his or her sexual orientation changes "quite quickly." He presents no evidence, of course, because there *isn't* any. Ralph Blair states that even so-called ex-gays have admitted "that the transformation does take a long, long time." [24] In reality, Blair has convincingly documented the fact that there is *no legitimate case in existence* of a true homosexual who has been successfully reoriented into a practicing heterosexual, Roberts' grandiose claim notwithstanding.

Finally, the faith-healing evangelist is reported to have told the tearful mother that he did not believe homosexuality is related to inborn tendencies. This conviction is not unique with Roberts. In fact, it is a cornerstone of fundamentalist presumption, for if it were ever firmly established that the sexuality of gay people was determined before their birth by circumstances beyond their control, they could not continue to accuse gays of being willful sinners without appearing cruel and vindictive. This they know, and it is not by chance that most homophobic Christian writers are solidly adamant in their stand that homosexuality is a conscious choice of the individual; that the person is ultimately responsible for his or her sexual conditioning. But as we have discussed earlier, most researchers and psychologists are convinced that homosexuality is *not* a freely chosen orientation, though they occasionally differ as to just how early in life homosexual orientation is developed. But what could be one of the most terrifying revelations of modern scientific research, in the minds of evangelical homophobes, is the very distinct possibility that both homosexual and heterosexual orientation are products of fetal brain development during pregnancy, and that both are very natural phenomena. More and more investigation is pointing in this direction.

A German scientist named Dorner has shown that gender and sex identity are primarily linked to neuroendocrinological (dealing with brain/hormone interactions) differences in brain development during the fourth to fifth months of fetal development for humans. Thus, both the *wiring* of the brain and the brain's sensitivity to the various sex hormones contribute to adult sexual behaviors and other sexual energy manifestations. . . .

The genetic transmission of homosexuality has been accepted for some time by geneticists and some psychologists. . . .

In sum, from the neurological, neuroendocrinological, genetic and physiological evidence, it can be stated that exclusive or nearly exclusive homosexuals have some amount of cross-sexed brain differentiation. When one looks at the behavioral and genetic groups, it is difficult to dispute the existence of a continuum of sexual brain development that plays a part in the manifestation of predominately male or female stereotypic sexual and/or gender behaviors. . . .

While there is little support for a theory of learning in relation to homosexuality, the part that learning plays in sexual behavior should not be underestimated. For those with initial cross-gendered neurological development, much heterosexuality must be learned. In cultures that prize heterosexuality and condemn homosexuality, it seems reasonable that many with initial cross-gendering would engage in denial of their own experience of their neurology. The denial of the basic sexual orientation and the sexual behavior normal to the individual, particularly for the highly condemned feminized or "sissy" boy may result in reality-based paranoia. In clinical practice, paranoia has been linked to a denial of homosexuality or inherent homosexual trends. However, not all paranoia is so linked, nor is homosexuality always a characteristic of paranoids.[25]

These few extracts, taken from a rather extensive thesis on the subject, give ample ammunition to those who have long been convinced that some of the roots of homosexuality are deeply embedded in the mysteries of biology. In light of the enormous strides being made in the field of genetic research with regard to sexual behavioral origins, evangelist Roberts and his peers should be advised to bite their lips, and be wisely reticent with their claims. Otherwise, they run the risk of looking like fools if more scientific evidence becomes conclusively contradictory of their pompous pronouncements on homosexual origins and "deliverance" possibilities.

This brief excursion into the inkwell of Christian homophobia, in all of its varied approaches has only scratched the surface of the excess of theological treatises consigning gay people to the ranks of the immoral, disobedient, rebellious, and demonically controlled enemies of the church. Some authors of these writings are so uninformed that they can inspire no more than pity and sadly humorous laughter. But taken collectively, there can be found a sinister thread of socially and religiously programmed prejudice against gay people weaving its way through many of these fundamentalist diatribes. Make no mistake: These books are literary guns, manufactured for the express purpose of killing the spirit of gay pride, dignity, and self-acceptance. The worst harm these works can perpetrate, however, is to reinforce the societal attitudes of fear, disgust, hatred, even violence against gay people—all renewed manifestations of that long-entrenched homophobia which in past centuries has so consistently plagued the Western mind.

It is imperative that we not underestimate the importance and sobering significance of conservative churchianity's latest homophobic book-binge. We are not dealing with the mere rantings of fringe fanatics whose self-inflated pronouncements are met with a public reaction, at most, of wry amusement. What is really frightening is the disturbing fact that the "faggot-burning" intolerance of Christian fundamentalism is becoming increasingly influential as a politically active force, seeking to remold the entire nation into a modified theocratic republic where separation of religion and state would be a thing of the past. The relentless lobbying of the Christian New Right (i.e., The Religious Round Table, Moral Majority, etc.) is beginning to take its toll as precious constitutional freedoms are being encroached upon by Leviticus-like legislation expressly aimed at the obliteration of all gay rights in housing and job opportunities, as well as social care.

Far from being harmless, the current inundation of local religious bookstores by the burgeoning distribution of anti-gay evangelical books is a sure signal that the poison of homophobic literature is fast becoming a staple of the conservative Christian's reading diet. Many Christian bookstores are gladly cooperating in this right-wing religious conspiracy by refusing to allow on their shelves any publications that are supportive of gay people or of a Christ-centered homosexual life-style. Those proprietors are apparently afraid that if their customers were exposed to both sides of the homosexual issue, they might begin to question past assumptions and even think for themselves, and that could be dangerous! It is a matter of record that out of the numerous books published in recent years on the controversy concerning homosexuality and the church, *very few* have been in any way supportive of the gay Christian position. This simply underscores the obvious: Gay persons in the Body of Christ constitute an over-whelmed and much maligned minority, and the continuing pub-licity given the horde of evangelical "exposés" of homosexuality can serve only to solidify the latent homophobic prejudice already permeating the conservative Christian establishment. With titles such as *The Gay Invasion* and *Shadow of Sodom* (to name but two), fearful and ignorant Christians are beginning to instill both theo-logical and psychological falsehood, thereby creating an atmosphere that could insure future ecclesiastical discrimination against the homosexual who is their neighbor. As militant homophobic Christians take up the cause, marching into spiritual battle against the enemy forces of the "gay invaders," they will no doubt have spectacular successes in their efforts to socially brainwash the average churchgoing mentality on the "evils" of homosexuality, but in the process, their army will have left the redeeming and accepting message of the Cross far behind.

NOTES

1. David Wilkerson and Don Wilkerson, *Counseling the Untapped Generation* (Grand Rapids: Zondervan Publishing House, 1971), pp. 119-20. Copyright © by Zondervan Publishing House. Used by permission. This permission applies to all succeeding quotations.
2. Sally Gearhart and William R. Johnson, *Loving Women/Loving Men: Gay Liberation and the Church* (San Francisco: Glide Publications, 1974, O.P.), p. 45, quoted from an article by Robert L. Treese. Used by permission. This permission applies to all succeeding quotations. Out of print.

3. Clinton R. Jones, *What About Homosexuality?* (Nashville/NewYork: Thomas Nelson, 1972), p. 13.

4. Wilkerson and Wilkerson, *Untapped Generation*; p. 120.

5. Frank Hammond and Ida Mae Hammond, *Pigs in the Parlor: A Practical Guide to Deliverance* (Kirkwood, Mo.: Impact Books, 1973), p. 142.

6. Gini Andrews, *Sons of Freedom: God and the Single Man* (Grand Rapids: Zondervan Publishing House, 1975), p. 131.

7. Martin Hoffman, *The Gay World* (New York: Basic Books, 1968), pp. 156-58.

8. C. A. Tripp, *The Homosexual Matrix* (New York: McGraw-Hill Book Co., Copyright © 1975 by Psychological Research Associates, Inc.), pp. 236-37. Used with the permission of McGraw-Hill Books, Co. This permission applies to all succeeding quotations.

9. Duane Pederson, *On Lonely Street With God* (New York: Hawthorn Books, 1973), pp. 151-61.

10. Paulette Hunnewell, answering questions based on her report for a graduate project/ thesis, "A Survey of Four Therapeutic Approaches to Male Homosexuality" (California State University, Northridge, 1974), submitted for partial fulfillment of the requirements for the degree of Master of Arts in Counseling & Guidance.

11. Bob Sutton, *Homosexuality: A Problem the Church Can No Longer Keep Outside Its Walls*, pamphlet (n.p., n.d.).

12. Tripp, *Homosexual Matrix*, pp. 73, n. 73-74.

13. *Awake!* (June 8, 1976), p. 11.

14. Tim LaHaye, *The Unhappy Gays* (Wheaton, Ill.: Tyndale House Publishers, 1978), p. 204. Used by permission.

15. The Jerusalem Bible, (Garden City, N.Y.: Doubleday & Co., 1966), Daniel 11:37, n.gg.

16. LaHaye, *Unhappy Gays*, p. 203.

17. Don Williams, *The Bond That Breaks: Will Homosexuality Split the Church?* (Los Angeles: BIM, 1978), p. 119. © Copyright 1978, BIM, Inc., Los Angeles, CA 90025. Used by permission. This permission applies to all succeeding quotations.

18. Ibid., p. 87.

19. Oral Roberts, *How to Get Through Your Struggles* (Tulsa, Okla.: Oral Roberts Evangelistic Association, 1977), pp. 142-43. Unfortunately, I am unable to reproduce the verbatim quote, since the Oral Roberts Evangelistic Association has refused to grant permission for it to appear in this book.

20. I have taken *theotherapeutic* in the context of its usage in Ralph Blair, *Holier-Than-Thou Hocus-Pocus and Homosexuality* (New York: HCCC, 1977), p. 26.

21. Ibid.

22. I use the term *mythic* here not in the popular sense of something fanciful and purely legendary, but in the scholarly usage which refers to ancient racial and cultural memories of real events, preserved through the process of literary idealization and parabolic symbolism.

23. Williams, *Bond That Breaks*, p. 53. Andy Comiskey, an "ex-gay" spokesperson for *Desert Stream*, "A ministry for homosexuals who seek to be new creatures in Christ" (according to their letterhead), heavily emphasizes this view. *Desert Stream* is headquartered in West Los Angeles, California.

24. Blair, *Holier-Than-Thou Hocus-Pocus*, p. 30.

25. Dean Gengle and Norman C. Murphy, "Revolutionary Extinction? An Emerging Model of the Origin of Sexualities," *The Advocate* (November 1, 1978), pp. 16, 19. Used by permission.

Chapter 4
Superstitions About the Scriptures

One of the difficulties often encountered by those of us who affirm the full acceptance of homosexuals into the church has been the assumption on the part of our opponents that in order to defend such a position, we must of necessity be denying the validity of biblical inspiration. This arises from the preconception that the psychological phenomenon of sexual inversion, which we today know as homosexuality, is identical with certain same-sex cultural practices repeatedly condemned in the Bible. Hence from the fundamentalist viewpoint, defending the legitimacy of the gay person's life-style is tantamount to contradicting what they consider to be "the Word of God." They argue that we of the gay community and our supporters cannot possibly be true Bible believers. We are accused of being religious renegades, seeking to undermine all credence and authority in the written Word of sacred tradition. But as this chapter will demonstrate, this accusation is without foundation. Actually, it is because of our opponents' tunnel-vision interpretation of Scripture that they accuse us of denying the Bible's inspiration. In truth, we are only repudiating faulty fundamentalist interpretation. Admittedly, there are different approaches within the Universal Church in regard to just exactly *how* the Bible was inspired, but none of those theological schools deny the wind of God's breath upon the pages of the holy Scriptures.

Generally speaking, there are two opposing theories concerning the nature of biblical inspiration.[1] The difference between them can be found by comparing these two sentences, which sum up their divergent approaches:

> The Bible contains the infallible message of
> the gospel and bears witness to the living
> Word of God.
>
> vs.
>
> The Bible *is* the infallible, inerrant Word
> of God.

It can easily be seen that this heated issue could create a yawning chasm that would separate Christians. At stake in this often divisive controversy is the scope, extent, and definition of the human/divine revelatory interaction. Does God's Word-communication with humankind express itself through mortal comprehension's fallible and imperfect perception? Or does the concept of God-breathed inspiration imply that human self-expression (such as speech and writing) is temporarily absorbed totally into the periphery of the infallible mind of God? Important theological implications are at issue. It is my personal feeling, after having studied much conflicting teaching, that the Word of God need not necessarily be equated with the written biblical record.

> The Bible is not the Word of God, but the words of men, in which and through which we believe the living, active, constantly contemporary Word of God comes to men. ... A Bible passage is to be interpreted in terms of the experiences, life setting and problems of the specific writer and with respect to the purposes for which it was written. ... A passage is to be further explicated in the light of our contemporary experience and knowledge. We must try to see it in relation to our social-psychological-historical-philosophical understanding as well as to our existential knowledge. ... Although the Bible writers faced the same basic existential questions we face, many of their answers are time-caught, as ours are, and valid only for them. But the values they affirmed by their answers are of significance to us. ... The whole Bible is to be seen in the light of the Gospel of Jesus Christ and the experience of the early Church.[2]

This position has much scriptural backing to commend it. It was Jesus who said to the Jewish fundamentalists of his day, "You search the Scriptures, because you think that in them you have eternal life; and it is these that bear witness of Me" (John 5:39 NASV). The holy Scriptures are not, in the truest sense, the Word of God, but they are the inspired written testimony *to* the living Word of God, who is none other than Jesus Christ himself; for as the apostle John most eloquently explained in the opening prologue to his Gospel; "The Word was made flesh, he lived among us, and we saw his glory, the glory that is his as the only Son of the Father, full of grace and truth" (John 1:14 JB). The Word of God was not made into a book, but into human flesh and bone. For this reason, it is often rightly contended that our veneration should not be focused upon the printed pages of sacred Scripture, but upon the nail-scarred hands of the One who tasted of our misery, limitations, fears, and simple joys. In his humanity, Christ's expression *(Word-bearing)* of the Godhead became complete. But it seems that many modern evangelicals and fundamentalists have created a theology centered around what could be called The Shrine of the Book—an idolatrous altar which countless believers have unwittingly set up in their hearts. Stone idols contain nothing of meaning beneath their sculptured surfaces—only the hardness of rock. In the same way, under the exterior of prominent bibliolatry, there exists nothing but stony literalism.

The Jews saw God's salvation as being embodied in the written text itself. Jesus warned them to readjust their focus. In a sense, they could not see the forest for the trees. In their obsession with every "jot and tittle" of the written Mosaic legacy, they had lost sight of its function as a prophetic arrow, pointing toward the Messiah in their midst. Their spiritual vision was so hampered by the blinders of "parchment preoccupation" that they were unable to discern the living Torah who walked among them.

Unfortunately, biblical fundamentalism has become a spiritual fetish among too many conservative Christians. Coined by one writer "the leaven of the Pharisees" against which Jesus had warned his disciples, literalism has been more often than not the last stronghold of racial prejudice and varied sociological superstitions; an open refuge for the last vestiges of a theological parochialism that should have disappeared with the Dark Ages.[3]

The Bible has profound significance as an historical and literary record of God's interaction with humanity and the revelation of God's will. When it is used to substantiate personal prejudices and self-righteous judgments, as it often is by literalists, its importance is diminished. ... A belief in biblical literalism is symptomatic of a person's failure or inability to exercise free will. The literalist betrays a fear of taking responsibility for her/his own life, decisions, and the consequences of those decisions. As long as there is an "absolute" (though clearly contradictory) listing of "dos and don'ts" to which one can profess to give allegiance (though no one has ever completely succeeded in doing so), one need not use one's own intelligence or manifest one's own faith. Blind allegiance to the biblical word is a denial of personal responsibility in relationship with God and with neighbor. Therefore, biblical literalism can in fact be declared to be idolatrous. ... Literalism is antithetical to the responsible life to which Jesus the Christ called his followers. It is also a denial of the continuing revelation of the Holy Spirit. ... Those who use certain ... passages from Paul's epistles as proof that God condemns Gay people are selective literalists. Their irresponsible use of Paul's writings gives evidence to their inability to cope with the reality of Gay love and Gay people and perhaps more often their inability to cope with sexuality and/or their own Gay feelings. Their homophobia, not their faith, is revealed.[4]

Anti-gay evangelicals, despite their denials, are characterized by theological inconsistency. No more perfect example could be found than their highly selective use of Paul's Epistle to the Romans. As we are already aware, it is the first chapter of Romans that is constantly hawked about as the New Testament's ultimate seal of doom upon any attempt to seek a position of open tolerance for homosexuality within the church. But when we examine the thirteenth chapter of Romans, we find that the fundamentalists and evangelicals have conveniently ignored Paul's plain and forthright teaching with regard to the divine right of governmental authority and the prohibition of any form of political or revolutionary insurrection. This submissive political policy is found in Romans 13:1-7.

You must all obey the governing authorities. Since all government comes from God, the civil authorities were appointed by God, and so anyone who resists authority is rebelling against God's decision, and such an act is bound to be punished. Good behavior is not afraid of magistrates; only criminals have anything to fear. If you want to live without being afraid of authority, you must live honestly and authority may even honour you. The state is there to serve God for your benefit. If you break the law, however, you may well have fear: the bearing of the sword has its significance. The authorities are there to serve God: they carry out God's revenge by punishing wrongdoers. You must obey, therefore, not only because you are afraid of being punished, but also for conscience' sake. This is also the reason why you must pay taxes, since all government officials are God's officers. They serve God by collecting taxes. Pay every government official what he has a right to ask—whether it be direct tax or indirect, fear or honour (JB).

Those who have been around conservative evangelicals for any length of time can testify that for the overwhelming majority, displaying patriotism for America and its system of government is considered to be participation in a holy cause—it becomes an extension of their religious duty to uphold "the American way." This self-imposed sense of responsibility has resulted in an extensive proliferation among conservative churches of rhetoric declaring that this country was founded as a Christian nation; that the ideals of the American Revolution must be preserved at all costs; and that our heritage of political freedom is a sacred privilege granted us by God, through our founding ancestors' valiant struggles against oppressive tyranny. To some of these propositions, I would concur. However, when the flowery myths of traditional American piety are dispelled by historical facts, and one then compares the Revolutionary ideals of 1776 with the religiopolitical philosophy of Paul in A.D. 63 (as recorded in Romans 13), one discovers that they could not be more diametrically opposed. Honest students of American history readily admit that many of the influential architects of the fledgling Revolutionary republic were far from being in the ranks of born-again Christianity. Many were Deists and intellectual rationalists.

The rallying battle cries of the American colonists were certainly not politically passive. They included such slogans as Liberty or Die, Don't Tread on Me, No Taxation Without Representation. That founding document of our liberty, the Declaration of Independence, specifically states that it is the duty and right of people to overthrow any government that is suppressive or tyrannical. But from Paul's perspective, "the divine right of kings" was clearly the political order established by God. In light of a literal interpretation of Romans 13:1-7, the American colonists who rebelled against the king of England were fighting against God's appointed authority, and their refusal to pay the demanded taxes was a flagrant act of unchristian insubordination worthy of punishment. Keep in mind that when Paul was writing his Epistle to the Romans, the government to which he was referring was that of the brutal and repressive Roman dictatorship of Nero. King George of England was a kitten by comparison!

So we see that by New Testament standards, a government's corruption and evil, or its denial of basic human rights and freedoms was not considered to be justification for rebellion. This creates a serious difficulty for most of the evangelical Christian patriotic propaganda which glorifies the origin of a system completely at odds with apostolic guidelines. This example is a splendid confirmation of the assertion that most fundamentalists and evangelicals are simply *selective* literalists with regard to biblical interpretation. This is especially evident in their insistence that Romans 1 must still be taken seriously today as a theologically valid, timeless, divine fiat on homosexual "depravity" (because they feel that the Bible should not be questioned, but primarily because of the overriding homophobic prejudice currently engendered by society). On the other hand, they often quote Romans 13 to condemn people like the draft evaders who would not serve their government during the Vietnam fiasco (fundamentalists identify with most right-wing establishment causes), but this same passage is conveniently ignored when its implications might discredit the popular American Revolutionary causes and the related folk heroes whose rebellion established our republic.

These observations have not been made to demean or belittle our country's historical or idealistic integrity, but simply to demonstrate that modern Christians have as much justification for questioning Paul's support of the divine right of governmental authority as gays have for disputing the validity of Paul's limited understanding of homosexuality. At least many gay Christians are honest enough to openly challenge the soundness of the apostle's presuppositions about the nature of homosexuality; while in marked contrast, the God-and-country evangelical wing of the church hypocritically proclaims its belief in the inerrancy of each of Paul's words, while they patriotically subscribe to a political philosophy that condones the necessity of revolution to secure the rights of oppressed people—a philosophy in total opposition to the apostolic guidelines of passive submission.

The inconsistency of fundamentalism's selective theological literalism has not escaped the notice of thoughtful Christian leaders, especially in reference to other aspects of Paul's teachings, which often cause perplexity among the ranks of the fundamentalist faithful.

> The major difficulty of Fundamentalism, by whatever name, is its inability to give an intelligible account of the Christian faith. ... Though many proclaim their Biblical literalism with confidence, it is soon evident, when we make careful inquiry, that the alleged literalism is actually held with reservations or with ambiguity. ... A good example of the problem which the literalist faces is that presented by the words of the Apostle Paul when he is definite on a number of subjects, such as the superiority of the unmarried state (I Cor. 7:7), and the subordination of women. How many are there, in fact, who accept without qualifications the assertion that, if there is anything women desire to know, "let them ask their husbands at home" (I Cor. 14:35)? If the literalist dismisses this unambiguous imperative by saying that it applied only to a particular situation, where there was a special problem of overtalkative women, he has already undermined his own general position. Much as we may admire the sincere devotion and sacrificial giving of many persons in the Fundamentalist camp, we must conclude that theirs is not a live option in the contemporary world.[5]

There is another principle of biblical interpretation that should not be overlooked, for it eliminates the necessity of attempting to apply to the twentieth century every opinion and pronouncement of the scriptural authors, as if they were agelessly appropriate.

Summarily stated, it is this: While the overall principles of God never change, the means of implementing them so that they are relevant to society often varies from age to age. Evangelicals fear the understanding that the eternal significance of the holy Scriptures has meaning in the context of culture, because this would undermine their faith-understanding of the Bible as being valid outside human circumstance. Their belief stands in ultimate contradiction, for example, to the fact that God chose to send the eternal Logos into a specific time and place through the Incarnation, allowing him to be conditioned and defined by the specific and existentially time-bound culture of first-century Judea.[6]

Our evangelical and fundamentalist accusers often assert that all the Bible is equally inspired, and therefore everything purporting to be an utterance from on High must be taken seriously. It is not our intention to disregard those pertinent biblical passages, but we prefer to place them in their proper perspective. Evidence from Scripture reinforces the assertion of many theologians that there is a continual thread of *progressive* revelation in the Bible, standing as a record of spiritual evolution in our understanding of the divine nature.

> Obviously, any idea of inspiration which implies equal value in the teachings of Scripture, or inerrancy in its statements, or conclusive infallibility in its ideas, is irreconcilable with such facts as this book presents. . . .
>
> There is no finality about it in the sense that the ideas which the Scriptures opened up were finished when the Scriptures stopped. Neither Judaism nor Christianity, despite their theories, has in practice succeeded in so treating the Book. . . . The God of the Bible has proved his quality as "the living God," who has not said his last word on any subject or put the finishing touch on any task. The supreme contribution of the Bible is not that it finished anything but that it started something. Its thinking is not so much a product as a process, issuing from a long precedent process and inaugurating an immeasurably important subsequent development. . . .
>
> So, the finalities of Scripture are mainly important because they are germinative. They are misinterpreted and misused when employed to stop further development rather than to encourage it.[7]

Therefore, for Christians to use the Bible as a dam to hold back the torrent of the Holy Spirit's continuous revelation through his common grace, operative through the behavioral sciences as well as through the various ministries in the Body of Christ that deal with contemporary issues of social, sexual, political, and ethical importance, amounts to nothing less than grieving the Spirit of God.

All this evidence would indicate that two-thousand-year-old concepts concerning homosexuality, among other things, cannot be considered final, flawless, or necessarily normative through the passing centuries, simply because they are found in the Bible. If we occasionally take issue with some of the plain assertions of Scripture, or demonstrate that some of its applications are archaic and incorrect, are we denying the inspiration of the Bible? Not at all! But divine inspiration is not a guarantee of infallibility.

> The Bible is a library of almost every kind of literary form, written or edited by fallible men whose inspiration did not exclude their looking through colored spectacles, or the limitations of the knowledge and outlook of the day in which they lived, or the party to which they belonged. . . .
>
> I am content to accept the criticisms which are perfectly valid about the Bible, and to make allowance for the human fallibility of those whose words have come down to me, and to secure which so many brave men have been willing to die. Criticisms of the Bible fall away as unimportant in those moments when, for all its fallibility and early crudity, some eternal truth blazes into vision and I catch a glimpse of God. I find repeatedly that I want to pray a very simple prayer:

> *Teach me to love Thy sacred word,*
> *And view my Saviour there.*[8]

Without a doubt, the Bible is uniquely inspired. It is inspired not simply on a level with any other uplifting literature, but much more so. The holy Scriptures are in a category by themselves; they are unique in their historical function as a written witness to the living God enfleshed in Jesus Christ. They are lofty expressions of faith, inspired by the Holy Spirit as an exemplary testimony, pointing toward and also documenting the fulfillment of the redemptive act of God in human history. Especially in the Scriptures of the

New Testament, we have a vividly woven word-tapestry of the way the living Lord, operating through the Spirit, invades our time-frame in order to jolt us into the reality of the spiritual, continually inspiring, sustaining, and guiding the Community of Faith through the ministries of the church.

In the writings of the Bible, preeminently in the Gospels and Epistles of early Christianity, we have had handed down to us a record of the basic truths and principles of New Testament faith, as understood and practiced *at that point in history*. It is highly doubtful that Paul had any idea that his letters would be preserved for almost two thousand years and treated as an extension of the holy Scriptures. Many of his Epistles dealt with specific situations as they occurred in the various local churches throughout Asia Minor and the rest of the Roman Empire. But it was the will of God, as history attests, to keep those writings for later generations, for within them, prophets, apostles, and martyrs witness to the reality of the Christ-event. They contain the basic foundational truths that are essential to the continuing expression of the Christian faith.

For one to question the inerrancy of the Bible is viewed by most evangelicals as a dangerous excursion into unbelief and a denial of what they consider to be the supreme authority for the church. There are several observations that should be made in relation to these reactions. First of all, the current debate in conservative theological circles regarding biblical infallibility is, when one gets to the bottom line, an absurdly irrelevant controversy. What most fundamentalists fail to take into consideration is that the Christian Church really has *no need* for an infallible Bible. They contend that if the Scriptures are mistaken in one area, then they cannot be trusted in anything they declare. Yet this fallacious logic would miserably fail the test of credibility, were we to measure our minis-ters, theological teachers, and spiritual leaders by the same yard-stick. Such perfectionist requirements, if applied to these people as to the Book from which they preach, would soon cause us all to lose faith in any human trustworthiness that falls short of absolute perfection. But most people will concede that an individual, to be considered trustworthy, does not require the quality of infallibility in matters of general knowledge, but only an honesty in communi-cating and acting upon the truth as he or she is able to perceive it. And there is no doubt in my mind that this is exactly what the authors of Scripture attempted to do. Peter, for instance, at various times in his ministry, was far from accurate in his understanding of God's purpose in certain perplexing situations in which Peter found himself.[9] This, however, did not invalidate the underlying revelations of the Gospel that he and the other apostles left indelibly imprinted upon the spirit of the church.

The Christian quest for biblical infallibility seems to be rooted in a kind of subconscious fundamentalist romanticism, which fantasizes a Bible unencumbered by its origin in the frail human response to the touch of the divine—a "close encounter," if you will, with the perfection of God. The New Testament Scriptures were written by men (and women?) who, just like contemporary fallible Christians, often fought with one another, misunderstood one another's teachings, and wrote emotional letters ranging from hot-tempered anger or cynical sarcasm to pure paeons of praise.[10] Whatever we find in the Scriptures, then, can be no more than a reflection of the transforming process of God's touch upon weak, unworthy, and *very* human earthen vessels (II Corinthians 4:7). That the Spirit of God truly moved upon the hearts and minds of the biblical authors is beyond question; but again, it must be emphasized that the Bible is a product of *human response* to the Spirit's leading. The holy Scriptures are not some kind of written theophany delivered to the apostles on a silver platter, untouched by human hands and surrounded by an aura of ethereal vision. As much as some Christians may wish to believe that the Bible was somehow dictated by a Chief Executive in the sky to his apostolic stenographers here below (who, of course, took perfect, inerrant shorthand), critical and responsible literary investigation cannot accept such a simplistic explanation without detriment to its academic integrity.

Contemporary evangelicals, charismatics, and fundamentalists who have fallen victim to an all-consuming obsession with the concept of biblical inerrancy (as demonstrated by Harold Lindsell and his *Battle for the Bible*), need to be reminded that the Scriptures do not speak as highly of themselves as do their "inerrantist" supporters. The most that Scripture does say about itself is that it is "profitable" for the purposes of teaching and moral correction (II Timothy 3:16) and that "whatever was written in earlier times was written for our instruction, that through perseverance and the encouragement of the Scriptures we might have hope" (Romans

15:4 NASV). Such modest statements concerning the sacred writings of our faith, *taken from those writings themselves*, are a far cry
from the lofty, if not almost worshipful fundamentalist claims of
unsullied perfection, which rival the naive piety of medieval
Marianism. There is no passage in the Bible in which its writings
are declared to be infallible. The only claim to inerrancy was made
by Paul—not for every word he uttered, but for the basic heart and
core of the gospel message itself:

> For I would have you know, brethren, that the gospel which
> was preached by me is not according to man. For I neither
> received it from man, nor was I taught it, but I received it
> through a revelation of Jesus Christ. (Galatians 1:11-12).
>
> Now I make known to you, brethren, the gospel which I
> preached to you, which also you received, in which also
> you stand, by which also you are saved, if you hold fast the
> word which I preached to you, unless you believed in vain.
> For I delivered to you as of first importance what I also
> received, that Christ died for our sins according to the
> Scriptures, and that He was buried, and that He was
> raised on the third day according to the Scriptures
> (I Corinthians 15:1-3).
>
> As we have said before, so I say again now, if any man is
> preaching to you a gospel contrary to that which you re-
> ceived, let him be accursed (Galatians 1:9 NASV).

As we can see, the gospel is a very simple, powerful, and con-
cise summation of the redemptive drama fulfilled in the risen
Christ. It does not establish a new Torah, complete with a multitude of regulations that must be meticulously observed with
legalistic minuteness. The gospel is the inerrant, freely flowing
declaration of grace to the world, which proclaims that enduring
love has triumphed with finality in Jesus Christ—a finality that
cannot be affected or deterred by the remnant of evil powers still
at work in the universe. The need for a divinely originated parchment, which demands of imperfect people a series of unattainable
requirements, was done away with at the Cross of Calvary (Colossians 2:14). The search for perfection, or infallibility, in writings,
codified commandments, or religious ceremonies constitutes only
an idolatrous lust for a tangible, physical idol—a "golden calf" that
can be erected in a misdirected attempt to dispel the dark shad-

ows of faithlessness and unbelief within ourselves. The Hebrews of old departed from their faith when Moses remained too long shrouded from sight atop the forbidding mountain of God's presence (Exodus 32:1-29). Similarly, there are multitudes of confessing Christians today who have transferred their focus of faith from Christ, who demands that our convictions be based upon those things that are not seen (Hebrews 11:1), to written words that can be seen, touched, memorized, and used in quasi-magical rituals of "proof texting" and "confessing the Word." For many of these adherents, the very idea of scriptural fallibility is traumatizing, since it suggests the possibility that much of their theology is like a house of cards—one good gust from the winds of sound academic or scientific inquiry, and the whole structure of literalistic fundamentalism could totter to its very foundations.

Actually, the concept of a Bible that is inspired, yet fallible, is a veritable tower of strength to Christians who are not afraid to face whatever truths the future may reveal, for the Scriptures then become an analogy in print of the Incarnation: the blending of the human and the divine into one united presentation of faith.

> I think it is important to clarify some basic issues. . . . The mystery . . . is that Almighty God would use imperfect words and people to convey eternal truth. It is that same mystery that we celebrate in the incarnation of the Word of God in Jesus Christ. It is part of God's love for us, that God allows Him/Herself to be revealed at all—and that the Eternal can be revealed in human words and human beings does not undermine God's authority, but exposes it for what it is: a function of *love*.[11]

Earlier in this chapter, the statement was made that the church has no real need for a doctrine of biblical inerrancy. To some who have been raised in more conservative Christian backgrounds, this no doubt is a rather astounding claim. But with a little logic and some unbiased, clearheaded thinking, one can quickly spot the circular trap into which scriptural infallibility proponents have unwittingly placed themselves. First, even if we were to concede that the Bible is inerrant and infallible, it would have absolutely no practical significance for the church or for the establishment of its dogmas. This conclusion arises from a most obvious but often overlooked fact: *An infallible Bible is of no value without an equally infallible interpreter.* The Roman Catholic Church long ago saw this fatal flaw in conservative Protestant theology, and to this day, Catholic literature aimed at the conversion of Protestants does not hesitate to make use of this philosophical problem. The Roman church has sought to solve the dilemma through its doctrine of papal infallibility. For Catholics, the pope is the one, final, and inerrant interpreter of the biblical tradition; he is called upon to decisively render theological judgments on essential faith and practice. However, the fact that this papal recourse has been used so seldom during the last century is an indication that even Catholics realize the precariousness of attributing to a human being the prerogative of divine infallibility, even in those rare instances when spoken *ex cathedra* from the papal throne.

For most fundamentalists, the answer to this problem is quite elementary: It is the Holy Spirit who is Scripture's infallible interpreter. They reason that since the Bible was inspired by the Spirit, it is only logical that the Spirit would be the best expounder of his own revelation. But alas, this seeming solution also falls prey to the relentless and consistent application of common sense. Even if the Bible were deemed to be inerrant and we were to concede that the Holy Spirit is its infallible interpreter, such a theological consensus still could have no real effect upon the Christian community, outside the realm of the purely abstract and academic. The existence of literally *hundreds* of Christian denominations throughout the world, each claiming to be teaching the most accurate version of the Truth, and each insisting that its biblical interpretations are the most correct, is powerful evidence that even though the Holy Spirit is the infallible interpreter of sacred Scripture, we Christians can at best only *imperfectly* perceive the flow of God's communication to us. This in turn leads us to one inescapable conclusion: If our perception of the Spirit's inerrant interpretation of the Bible can be received only through the darkened glass of human fallibility (I Corinthians 13:12), then the whole concept of biblical infallibility becomes a moot and pointless issue.

So many fundamentalists fail to understand that God's inspiration is inerrant *only* at its source, within the depths of the originating mind of Deity; that its revelation to us finite, time-bound creatures can be accomplished only by a transliteration of the pristine Light of the divine omniscience into that flickering candle flame within the human spirit, which strives to communicate the

wisdom of ultimate Truth through the intricate and frequently
tangled mesh of our Adamic psyches. Like brilliant shafts of golden
sunlight piercing through the defenses of a dark and stormy
cloudbank, so is the nature of God's refracted revelation as it filters
through the darkened ignorance of human misunderstanding, until at last occasional glimmering light-rays of inspiration break
through the gray canopy of misperception that often clouds the
accuracy of our awareness in the realm of Spirit. Nor has this truth
been lost to certain of the more sensitive and reflective Christian
writers. Michael J. Christensen, in his short but excellent *C. S.
Lewis on Scripture*, examines the interpretations of that famed
theologian regarding the nature of scriptural inspiration and
comes to a similar conclusion.

While I often found myself at odds with some of his theological
views, I feel that the late Episcopal Bishop James A. Pike contributed a very insightful commentary concerning the Bible's supposed infallibility.

> Contemporary Fundamentalists, whose strongest forte is
> not church history, maintain that the Church is founded on
> the Bible. The plain fact is that the foundation of the people
> of the Old Covenant (Covenant = Testament) preceded the
> writings and official selection of the Old Testament; and the
> Church of the New Covenant was in existence quite a while
> before the writing in the official adoption of the anthology
> known as the New Testament. Abraham did not arrive at
> Beersheba with a copy of the Pentateuch in his luggage;
> Paul did not distribute pocket Testaments on his mission-
> ary journeys. In this regard, the Catholic Churches (in the
> narrower usage—Roman, Eastern Orthodox, and Anglican)
> have the better case: the Bible is the Church's book. The
> Bible has no greater authority than the many persons, writ-
> ers and editors, acting individually as transmitters of oral
> tradition, and acting individually or corporately as eccle-
> siastical officials. Unless they are infallible—all of them—
> the Bible is not infallible. . . . In short, to view the Bible as
> the infallible norm is necessarily either to attribute finality
> to the many persons who put the Bible together *or* to make
> an act of faith in the Bible directly without any underpin-
> nings for the affirmation.[12]

The problem of so many evangelical Christians today centers around their insistence that the Bible is the *supreme* authority on all matters of spiritual and moral consequence. This, however, was not the case in the early Christian community. The Scriptures were not viewed as *the* authority, but rather as *supplementary and corroborating* authority. To be sure, the sacred writings of the prophets and apostles were valued highly as being "profitable" for spiritual growth and teaching, but the Supreme Head of the church was and is Jesus Christ himself. He manifests his author-itative guidance by the Holy Spirit through the medium of Scrip-ture and also through the foundational and teaching ministries that have arisen within the Universal Church in every generation (Ephesians 1:22-23, 4:11-16). The church's bond of unity and faith-fulness to Christ is kept constant and alive, not through a slavish preoccupation with biblical literalism, but through the recognition of the presence of God's Spirit at work in the Body of Christ—the Spirit who can no more be constrained by the strictures of narrow-minded Bible thumpers than can the wind (John 3:8).

Keeping all these things in mind, it would be well for us to see how the apostle Paul admonished the churches to interpret the inspired messages that came through persons in the local assem-blies who spoke under the anointing of the gift of prophecy: "Do not stifle inspiration, and do not despise prophetic utterances, *but bring them all to the test and then keep what is good in them and avoid the bad of whatever kind*" (I Thessalonians 5:19-22 NEB [emphasis mine]). In this passage, Paul has given us a key to the interpretation of the entire body of Scripture, for just as prophetic utterance is the inspired speaking of truth through a human chan-nel, the Bible is a collection of inspired writings brought forth through human instrumentality. In either case, we are told to bring it to the test, accepting the obviously inspired portions, but being careful to reject any judgmental errors or archaic social attitudes that may not be consistent with our present understand-ing of the Christian gospel. This is the only way we can "accurately handle the word of truth" (II Timothy 2:15), and it can be done only through the aid of the Holy Spirit within us, for he is the Anointing who is to teach us all things and lead us into all Truth, to the extent that our human perception of God will allow (John 16:13; I John 2:20-21).

Our examination of the nature, place, and purpose of the holy

Scriptures has been important, for it has aptly demonstrated why exception must be taken to the fundamentalist battle cry that the Bible *is* the Word of God (without any qualifications). If we allow such a basic and error-filled presupposition to go unchallenged, the homophobic evangelicals and others of their ilk will never give a second thought to their smugly confident assumption that since the Bible is perfect in every part, there can be no doubt that homosexuals are idol-worshiping, child-molesting, sex-crazed perverts of the lowest order. Gay people, of course, know better. But until the myths and superstitions about the supposed magical omniscience of the biblical Scriptures are dispelled by the truth of responsible theological scholarship, there will continue to be a mass of "true believers," angrily waving Bibles that they do not understand, in defiance of homosexual acceptance.

NOTES

1. There are actually more than two schools of thought with regard to biblical inspiration. There are numerous shades of interpretation in between the two extremes I have illustrated. For an excellent overview of the inspiration/inerrancy debate, see Stephen T. Davis, *The Debate About the Bible*, (Philadelphia: Westminster Press, 1977).
2. Sally Gearhart and William R. Johnson, *Loving Women/Loving Men: Gay Liberation and the Church* (San Francisco: Glide Publications, 1974, o.p.) p. 28.
3. Clyde E. Fant, *Preaching for Today* (New York: Harper & Row, 1975), pp. 30-33.
4. Gearhart and Johnson, *Loving Women/Loving Men*, p. 104.
5. Elton Trueblood, *The Future of the Christian* (New York: Harper & Row, 1971), pp. 68-69.
6. John 1:1-18; Galatians 4:5; Luke 2:51-52.
7. Harry Emerson Fosdick, *A Guide to Understanding the Bible* (New York: Harper & Row, Torchlight Books, 1938), pp. xiv-xv.
8. Leslie Weatherhead, *The Christian Agnostic* (Nashville: Abingdon Press, 1965), pp. 198, 201.
9. See Acts 10; Galatians 2.
10. Regarding church in-fighting, see Acts 15:36-40; Galatians 2:11-14. An example of possible doctrinal misunderstanding can be seen in a comparison of James 2 with Romans 3, 4. For an overview of apostolic anger and cynicism, one should refer to II Corinthians 10, 11, 12. Probably one of the finest examples of inspired praise can be found in Ephesians 3.
11. Nancy Wilson, "By What Authority?" *The Gay Christian* (May 1976), p. 7 (A Journal of Theological Reflection from Metropolitan Community Church).
12. James A. Pike, *If This Be Heresy* (New York: Dell Publishing Co., A Delta Book, 1967), pp. 47-48.

Chapter 5
Hebrew History and Homosexuals

M uch fundamentalist Christian literature may seek to discredit and damn the gay Community of Faith for teaching or practice, but there are no authentic grounds for denying our incorporation into the universal Body of Christ. For we, too, recognize the Lordship of Jesus Christ, the inspiration of the holy Scriptures, and the regenerating work of the Spirit in the world today. The contention is often raised that gay people are violating the plain admonitions of the Hebrew Scriptures against the practice of homosexuality. The problem here is in ascertaining exactly what those writings actually say on this subject, and in arriving at an understanding of the implications those statements have for us today, based upon the historical and social contexts of the times in which they were written. As long as these avenues of investigation are left unexplored, an adequate insight into this controversy is impossible.

Without question, the Old Testament condemns homosexual acts between men (women are not mentioned in this context): "You shall not lie with a man as with a woman: that is an abomination. . . . If a man has intercourse with a man as with a woman, they both commit an abomination. They shall be put to death; their blood shall be on their own heads" (Leviticus 18:22; 20:13 NEB). However, it is essential that we try to understand the various reasons that prompted such prohibition. It has been suggested by some gay theologians, in their early attempts to defend the homosexual position, that an underlying motive for forbidding same-sex activity was its inability to procreate. Barrenness was very often considered a disgrace in ancient Israel (Deuteronomy 7:14). Going further, we find recorded in Genesis 38:9-10 the story of Onan, who refused to complete intercourse with his dead brother's wife so that there would be no offspring to carry on his brother's name and inheritance. This was an intentional violation of ancient Hebrew leviratic laws, and in the words of the Genesis account, the Lord was so displeased that he took Onan's life. This reveals a strong undercurrent, reflecting displeasure toward anything that would prevent or interfere with procreation. Fewer children meant fewer fighting men and almost certain extinction for the early patriarchs and their tribal clans, surrounded as they were by a multitude of hostile nations. From this perspective, it is easy to see why a homosexual act would be unlawful under the Israelite economy, for it was simply another form of sexual activity that would eliminate any possibility of procreation—a "wasting of the seed." This postulation is, no doubt, intriguing, but there is little evidence that such was the substance of Hebrew reasoning. In all probability, it was a contributing cause for such levitical enactments, but little more.

Another explanation—one with much historical backing—has to do with the extremely sexist attitudes of Hebrew patriarchal society, which placed women in a most degrading light, therefore creating a homophobic abhorrence for any kind of sexual activity where a man was seemingly "feminized" by taking a passive sexual position with another man.

> The entire socio-cultural functioning of the ancient Israelites was wrapped up in the radical separateness and inequality of the sexes. To refuse to observe such distinctions between the sexes either by a man's dressing in the accepted apparel of the opposite sex or by participation in sexual relations which appeared to substitute another man for a woman was, of course, strictly taboo within these cultural outlooks.[1]

Even more important is the fact that homosexual acts were often associated with heathen idolatry, therefore a violation of the first table of the Decalogue and worthy of death. Some of the pagan religions of the cultures surrounding Israel often included homosexual acts as part of their rituals. Sacred cult prostitution was prevalent even among the Israelites during times of national apostasy and was vigorously condemned by the prophets.[2] The association of homosexual acts with idol worship has recently gained more widespread acceptance among biblical scholars, including Martin Noth and Norman Snaith, in their respective commentaries.[3] However, evangelical author Don Williams has taken issue with this conclusion. He feels that Leviticus 18:22 cannot be explained away as merely a prohibition against idolatrous behavior:

> There is no reason to suppose that homosexual behavior endangered Hebrew morals and that the law against homosexual acts was designed to combat idolatry. The fact is that this law, "You shall not lie with a male as with a woman," clearly and simply prohibits male homosexual relations. . . .
>
> There is, unfortunately, no evidence for this assertion [that references to homosexual prohibitions were in the context of cultic prostitution]. . . . Furthermore, the use of males in a fertility cult is absurd.[4]

Unfortunately for Williams, even fellow anti-gay exegete Kenneth Gangel admits the extensive existence of sacred male homosexual prostitution throughout the ancient Canaanite cultures of that time period.[5] It is therefore hard to believe that the levitical Code of Holiness, which was so concerned for cultic purity and separation from idolatrous practices, would ignore such a well-known practice in its list of condemnations. Williams also feels that the suggestion of homosexual male prostitutes in a heterosexually oriented fertility cult is preposterous. However, Tom Horner, in his detailed study of homosexuality in the Old Testament era clarifies this seeming inconsistency when he describes the religious and sexual customs of the emasculated priests of Cybele. He gives an excellent description of the use of male prostitutes in a fertility cult, and his explanation establishes that it is *not* absurd.

> Like the dedicated women, these men [sacred cult prostitutes] were also in the service of the goddess and, *in a sense, were even more dedicated in that they had made a greater sacrifice: they had offered to the goddess their manhood.* [After describing their ritual of voluntary self-castration, Horner continues.]

The average male worshiper, however, was not that devoted. . . . That the men would indirectly offer their seed to
the goddess through the direct medium of the sacred male
prostitute was the next step. Intercourse with these devotees who had made the supreme sacrifice of their manli-
ness to the goddess *could have been considered more
efficacious than a similar act with a female temple function-
ary* (emphasis mine).[6]

In further support of the theory that the Leviticus homosexual
prohibitions stem in large part from their relatedness to pagan
idolatry is the nature of the Hebrew word translated *abomination*
when referring to same-sex acts. John Boswell makes the important observation that

the Hebrew word "toevah" . . . here translated "abomination," does not usually signify something intrinsically evil,
like rape or theft . . . but something which is ritually unclean for Jews. . . . It is used throughout the Old Testament
to designate those Jewish sins which involve ethnic con-
tamination or idolatry. . . . Often "toevah" specifically means
"idol," and its connection with idolatry is patent even within the context of the passages regarding homosexual acts.[7]

This is not the only Mosaic passage that condemns homosexual acts in the context of idolatrous sexuality. In Deuteronomy
23:17-18, we find a reference to both heterosexual and homosexual
sacred cult prostitution.

There must be no sacred prostitute among the daughters of
Israel, and no sacred prostitute among the sons of Israel.
You must not bring to the house of Yahweh your God the
wages of a prostitute or the earnings of a dog, whatever vow
you have made, for both are detestable to Yahweh your
God (JB).

Dog is a derogatory designation for a sacred homosexual prostitute, as a casual examination of some of the more recent scholarly
commentaries will confirm.[8] At this point, it is necessary to briefly
examine a New Testament passage that some homophobic Christians consider to be related. It should be remembered that most
fundamentalists make use of some of the older, less accurate, and

more misleading translations that do not use the terminology
male cult prostitute in Deuteronomy 23:17, but the greatly misunderstood *sodomite* instead. In our society this term has taken
on the meaning of *homosexual* in a generalized sense—a meaning
the original Hebrew word does not convey, as many of the modern
Bible versions make plain. The precise interpretation of the word
was linked specifically to cultic sexual idolatry, not homosexual
activity in general, something of which most uninformed evangelicals are not even remotely aware. Because of this misunderstanding, many homophobic Christians have been led to believe that
dog is a scriptural reference to homosexuals generally. As a result,
it is the contention of some fundamentalists that Jesus himself
condemned homosexuals and damned them to exclusion from
the City of God in Revelation 22:14-15. The passage in question
reads as follows:

> Happy are those who . . . will have the right to feed on the
> tree of life and can come through the gates into the city.
> These others must stay outside: dogs, fortune-tellers, and
> fornicators, and murderers, and idolaters, and everyone of
> false speech and false life (JB).

In the previous verse (13), it was Jesus himself who was speaking,
for he identified himself as the One who is coming again, and as
the Alpha and Omega. In verse 16, Jesus is continuing to speak, for
it begins, "I, Jesus, have sent My angel." Therefore it is not unwarranted to assume that verses 14 and 15 are a continuation of his
dialogue with John. Since the words are those of Jesus, it would be
best to interpret them by his own remarks which make use of the
same terminology elsewhere in the Gospels. Just what did he
mean by *dogs*? Whatever Jesus meant, it will immediately become
apparent that in regard to Revelation 22:15, the burden to prove
that *dogs* refers to the same class of persons condemned in
Deuteronomy 23:17 rests squarely on the shoulders of our fundamentalist detractors. As mentioned before, Jesus is the best interpreter of his own words. Where else then, do we find Jesus
speaking of people in terms of lowly *dogs*? The answer is found in
the Gospel of Matthew: "Do not give dogs what is holy; and do not
throw your pearls in front of pigs" (7:6, JB). By no stretch of the
imagination can it be inferred that our Lord is making reference to
homosexuals here, for in this same Gospel he uses the diminutive

form of this term when referring to Gentiles (15:26). This was a common practice among the Jews of that time in describing non-Jews. It is plain from Matthew 7:6 that Jesus is speaking in a symbolic way of disbelieving infidels, *not* gay people.

It is interesting to note that there are a variety of ways in which the scriptural writers employed the metaphoric *dog*. The prophet Isaiah called the unscrupulous members of the religious establishment of his day "dumb and greedy dogs" (Isaiah 56:10-11). Paul followed the prophet's example when he accused the false teachers who preached circumcision as a prerequisite for salvation of being "dogs to beware of" (Philippians 3:2). In the same verse he called them mutilators, a deprecation of their insistence on circumcision. Ironically, it is those homophobic ministers of today, the paragons of the right-wing religious establishment, who are mutilating the Scriptures, twisting them out of context in order to make the gay people of this nation scapegoats for all the social ills of society and the breakdown of the nuclear family. It is their firm conviction that we must circumcise our sexuality, either by forced celibacy, repression of our urges, or by heterosexual marriage in order to be accepted by God as authentic Christians. Actually, it is they who are the modern "dogs" outside the holy place of God's approval. They are the disbelievers of God's acceptance of gay people, the pompous and self-righteous preachers of hate and prejudice against a sexual minority of the Lord's creation that they do not understand, or simply do not *want* to understand. Just who are these rabidly homophobic canines? One need only turn the controls of the television to hear their vicious barkings on Sunday morning—prime-time evangelists and others in the pack of pseudo-spiritual "dogs," barking their gospel of theocratic fascism and social intolerance. But one thing can be established beyond doubt: Jesus' final words to us in the book of Revelation are not a put-down of our sexuality as gay people. In fact, they could more appropriately be interpreted as a reference to the vicious mentality of those who, like lowly curs, have turned on the loving message of their Master, assuming an attitude of total hostility toward the people described by Jesus as the "least of these my brothers and sisters" (Matthew 25)—gays, blacks, and other minorities, as well as those religious visionaries who trouble the conscience of the established church.

When one reviews the probable motivations behind the prohibitions of homosexual acts in the levitical Holiness Code, it is clearly evident that the evils of temple cult prostitution have no relevance whatever as a valid excuse for condemning homosexual inversion in present-day society. Such scriptural proscriptions are patently anachronistic; their chief value lies in the archaeological and historical insight they provide regarding the life-styles and the cultural conflicts faced by the early Hebrews in their struggles with the surrounding Canaanite society. Certainly, for Christians to appeal to an ancient law code which institutionalized the patriarchal, sexist notions of male domination, with its resulting homophobia echoed in these levitical precepts, is to align themselves with the demeaning convictions of male chauvinism. Moreover, to utilize these passages from Scripture as an indication of divine displeasure with nonprocreative sexuality is to create a double-edged sword that will surely impale our accusing, birth-control practicing, fundamentalist friends! With the burgeoning population explosion and growing world famine, it would be absurd to demand that we take the original Genesis injunction to multiply as a timeless precept which God meant to remain applicable. We now realize that sexuality serves many higher functions than reproduction: the expression of intimate love, the affirmation of the worth of the beloved, and the strengthening of the bonds of relationship.

The pick-and-choose attitude of fundamentalist Christians toward Old Testament Law is indefensible. Their patchwork handling of the Mosaic legal system is neither justifiable nor honest. Evangelicals often take certain passages from the Torah that forbid homosexual activity, isolating them from the context of the Law as a whole. It is truly amazing that they actually have the audacity to use these texts as an indication of God's continuing anger and opposition toward gay people and homosexuality, while they conveniently ignore a host of other Scripture passages which condemn, in no uncertain terms, many things that are an integral part of their own daily life-style. A few examples from the Pentateuch should make the hypocrisy of this homophobic theology abundantly clear.

"The man who lies with a woman during her monthly periods and uncovers her nakedness ... both of them must be outlawed from their people" (Leviticus 20:18 JB). How many Christian heterosexual couples have violated this prohibition? The verdict of Leviticus: Outlaw them from the church!

"You are not to round off your hair at the edges nor trim the edges of your beard" (Leviticus 19:27 JB). Modern hairstyling would certainly suffer catastrophic losses on the heels of such a prohibition. Barbers beware!

> You must eat nothing with blood in it.
> The pig must be held unclean. . . . You must not eat the meat of such animals.
> Anything in sea or river that has not fins or scales, of all the small water-creatures and all the living things found there, must be held detestable. . . . You are not to eat their flesh (Leviticus 19:26;11:7-8,10-12 JB).

There goes rare steak, juicy prime rib, ham, bacon, pork chops, shrimp, lobster, clams, scallops, and oysters!

"You must not wear clothing woven part of wool, part of linen" (Deuteronomy 22:11 JB). Say good-bye to the modern clothing industry's advances in synthetic and combined materials!

Of course, these are just some of the shorter, less elaborate commandments. Provisions were made also for the institution of slavery (Leviticus 25:44-46). Wars of total extermination, which could easily have rivaled Herod's massacre of the innocents in Bethlehem, were often commanded (so much for humanitarian sensitivity) (Deuteronomy 20:16-17). Parents could have their children legally stoned to death for disobedience (Deuteronomy 21:18-21). Blood revenge and trial by ordeal were also part of that same Mosaic legacy (Exodus 21:23-25; Numbers 35:19, 26-27; 5:11-31). The list could go on ad infinitum.

Obviously, one would be a fool not to admit that the Old Testament ethic leaves much to be desired as a workable standard in a modern Christian society. This is not hard to understand when we realize that ancient Israel was a semibarbaric society, struggling to survive in a brutal world where human life was a cheap commodity. Much that was considered morally acceptable in biblical times, we would consider immoral, or at least sub-Christian by our present standards of morality and ethics.[9] We should also remember that an activity or custom deemed to be indecent in that era, due to various cultic regulations, may well be considered permissible in most contemporary cultures.

When Christians point to the ancient Law of Moses as proof of gay sinfulness, it must mean that they still recognize the Law as being valid and a norm for modern believers. However, if it is to be enforceable against gays, it must of necessity be applicable to fundamentalists as well; so since they have placed themselves under the Law, they have obviously deserted the provisions of grace made possible through the liberating gospel of Jesus Christ, which insists that we are no longer under obligation to the old Law, but are freed to serve God in the responsible freedom of grace and forgiveness (Romans 6:14; Galatians 3:10-14).

Before going on to reflect upon the attitudes of the New Testament writers, we must not fail to examine the notorious saga of Sodom and Gomorrah. The ancient account of their destruction can no longer be used as a blanket condemnation of homosexuality, as has been assumed by such religious opponents as Kenneth Gangel, author of a book titled *The Gospel and the Gay* (endorsed on the cover by Anita Bryant). Printed on the back leaf of the book is this incredibly uninformed assertion: "We know of only one episode in history where God singled out a particular sin and destroyed two entire cities because of it—the sin was homosexuality and the cities were Sodom and Gomorrah." [10]

It is not surprising that the Bible denies Gangel's claim in at least three places. Genesis 18:20-21 indicates that God had planned the destruction of those cities for their wickedness *long before* the incident at Lot's house took place. In addition, in Genesis 19 is the *only* reference to an attempted perpetration of a homosexual act by the men of Sodom. In light of this, Gangel's sweeping accusation that "sexual recreation was rampant in the city to the point that gay crowds roamed the streets demanding sexual relations with every stranger who visited town" seems strange indeed.[11] His statement sounds as though it is an eyewitness account, a feat hardly conceivable unless, per chance, Gangel is a believer in reincarnation who thinks himself to be remembering a past life—in Sodom! To magnify one isolated incident into the "primary" sin the two cities had committed is exaggeration taken to its limits—an exaggeration supported nowhere but in the lurid imaginations of homophobic Christians. Included in the *scriptural* list of Sodom's sins are pride of wealth, affluence, lack of concern for the poor, haughtiness, adultery, and other sins in general (Ezekiel 16:49; Jeremiah 23:14). Homosexuality is not mentioned!

Most evangelical and fundamentalist authors vehemently condemn homosexuality as inherently sinful on the basis of this Genesis account, which describes a scene of attempted *rape* of angelic messengers by male Sodomites. The correlation is totally unacceptable. In the first place, to condemn heterosexuality, for example, because of the increase of heterosexual rape is patently ridiculous. Second, the fact that the men of Sodom were seeking to molest the two strangers does not prove them to be true homosexuals or "gay crowds." What it *does* prove is that they were depraved, degenerate, and lustful, with violent intentions. It does *not* prove that they were, by any stretch of the imagination, what we would today call constitutional homosexual inverts.

The fact that the men of Sodom refused Lot's offer of his daughters does not, as some Christian writers have claimed, indicate that they were homosexuals in the fullest sense of the word. Two evangelical authors, Virginia Ramey Mollenkott and Letha Scanzoni, in their excellent book *Is the Homosexual My Neighbor?: Another Christian View*, give us an illuminating insight into the *real* reason for the Sodomites' refusal to sexually abuse the daughters of Lot:

> Among some ancient peoples, it was not unusual to flaunt one's triumph over enemies by treating them with the greatest possible contempt. Such contempt was demonstrated by forcing captive men to "take the part of a woman" and be passive recipients in anal intercourse.
>
> A similar pattern shows up in modern prisons. "We're going to take your manhood" or "We're gonna make a girl out of you" are common assertions in such sexual assaults. . . .
>
> If the modern prison's version of a gang rape was in the minds of the men of Sodom, it is understandable that they did not accept Lot's offer of his daughters. Women already had a low place in the society of Sodom (Lot's offer is indicative of that fact). Humiliating actual women would not have provided the sense of conquest they had anticipated in degrading the male strangers and "dragging them down" to the level of women.[12]

Seen in this light, there is no concrete evidence that the men of Sodom were homosexual in the sense of true sexual inversion. Furthermore, the focus of condemnation here is upon gang rape, not sexual orientation. Some paranoid evangelicals have used the

Sodom account and a similar narrative in Judges 19 as an indication of the general nature of homosexuals. After discussing these
two passages, Gangel comes to the absurd conclusion that "this
kind of passage should deliver us once and for all from the notion
that homosexuals by and large are just a nice quiet group of people who want to be left alone to 'do their own thing.' " [13] In other
words, he implies that most gay people are potential child molesters and violent mob-oriented rapists! Echoes of the Anita myths
are still very much in vogue with ostrich-headed Christians who
refuse to allow themselves to be confronted with statistics and
facts. Further examples of evangelical paranoia can be found in the
sensational "visions" of David Wilkerson.

> Believe me when I tell you the time is not far off that you
> will pick up your local newspaper and read sordid
> accounts of innocent children being attacked by wild
> homosexual mobs in parks and on city streets.... I see
> them coming in our generation. [14]

Interviewed in a nationally distributed periodical, psychologist
Norman C. Murphy refuted the slanderous assertions of both
Gangel and Wilkerson.

> When you read about a homosexual rape in the news,
> almost invariably it was the rape of a homosexual by a
> group of heterosexuals. In prison populations, heterosex-
> uals often gang rape young prisoners and homosexuals....
> Violent sex crimes are the province of heterosexuals in
> almost all instances. When you look at the number of
> homosexuals and heterosexuals with regard to violent sex-
> ual assaults, there is no comparison. Heterosexuals win the
> prize for being rapists and murderers when the numbers of
> such felons are measured within the homosexual and
> heterosexual populations....
>   The news media always makes a big thing about a
> homosexual's murdering someone. The general population
> often believes that homosexuals as a group are murderers.
> Further, often the so-called homosexual murder was a
> murder committed by a heterosexual with the homosexual
> as victim. [15]

Of further interest is the fact that in their attempt to portray gay people as possessing the demented nature of violent rapists, most fundamentalists and evangelicals will emphasize the murderous cruelty perpetrated by the men of Gibeah in the book of Judges. That is the tragic story of degenerates who surrounded an old man's house and demanded to have sexual relations with the man who was his guest for the night. In desperation, the guest threw out to them his concubine, who in turn was gang-raped outside the house all through the night. The next morning, she was found dead at the doorway. To place the label homosexual upon the men of Gibeah betrays gross ignorance bordering on the absurd. Gay people are not sexually attracted to the opposite gender. That simple point of information should be the basic building block in understanding the nature of homosexuality. But it seems that this fundamental fact has somehow escaped the attention of the fundamentalists, for who could conceive of male homosexual inverts raping a woman all night long? We know, of course, that rape is primarily an act of violence, but that act is nearly always expressed within the parameters of the rapist's sexual orientation, except in those cases of heterosexual prison confinement, where there is a lack of intimacy with the opposite sex. As has already been stated, it is not uncommon to hear that a homosexual man was raped by heterosexual men for the purpose of violent humiliation. But the incidence of gay people raping a heterosexual is, like the proverbial needle in the haystack, virtually nonexistent. In the final analysis, we should not dignify the men of Gibeah with the appellation of either heterosexual or homosexual; there is only one accurate description of them: sexual degenerates. Judges 19 is no more authentic in reference to true homosexual inversion than is Genesis 19 and its account of Sodom.

The only other biblical passage that has influenced the interpretation of the Sodom story is the seventh verse in the Epistle of Jude. Unfortunately, many modern Bible versions have contributed toward an erroneous understanding of this verse by using the phrase "unnatural lusts," as does, for instance, The New English Bible.

> Remember Sodom and Gomorrah and the neighbouring towns; like the angels, they committed fornication and followed unnatural lusts; and they paid the penalty in eternal fire, an example for all to see.

Actually, the King James Version comes closer to the meaning of the original Greek: "giving themselves over to fornication, and going after *strange flesh*" (emphasis mine). The hideousness of the Sodomites' sin was not so much the *nature* (homosexual or heterosexual) of the sexual act which the men at Lot's house may have wanted to perform. The writer of that episode focuses instead upon the fact that those men were so base and demented as to seek the violent sexual humiliation of *angels*, divine beings of a higher order. This was no doubt due to their sinful degeneracy, which blinded their ability to perceive the presence of the Holy within their midst. (Having lost any sense of spiritual discernment, the men of Sodom were probably suspicious that the strangers were spies, whom they looked forward to capturing and subsequently abusing in sexual humiliation as a preliminary to an even worse fate.) This is the primary thrust of Jude's argument. The "homosexuality" of the incident is probably not being referred to at all.

Paul, in his detailed explanation of the meaning of resurrection, made a statement about the comparative nature of physical flesh which conclusively demonstrates that the term "strange flesh" must be a reference to flesh that is *other than human* (i.e., possibly angelic).

> All flesh is not the same flesh, but there is *one flesh* of men, and another flesh of beasts, and another flesh of birds, and another of fish. There are also heavenly bodies and earthly bodies, but the glory of the heavenly is one, and the glory of the earthly is another (I Corinthians 15:39-40 NASV, [emphasis mine]).

If, as Paul says, all humans are of the same flesh, then homosexual activity could not be described as going after "strange" flesh. On the other hand, bestiality *could* be so described, for beasts are of another flesh, according to the biblical viewpoint; so, also, would lusting after spiritual beings whose "flesh" is of a different nature and composition than that of human beings, and this is exactly what occurred in Genesis 19. It is not homosexuality that is the primary issue for Jude; it is rather the debased audacity of sinful human creatures who attempted to attack and humiliate the very messengers of the living God.

In this brief overview of the Old Testament Scriptures and their proper interpretation in regard to homosexuality, one point has become very clear: The Bible passages used by homophobic religionists in their attempts to consign gay people to damnation are not in the least intimidating when carefully examined in the light of cultural and historical context. And more important, when they are scrutinized in the awareness of our New Covenant relationship with Jesus Christ, which has liberated us from the legalistic bondage of the Old Testament, it is evident that gays have nothing to fear from the God who gave his only begotten Son to die for their redemption.

NOTES

1. Ralph Blair, *An Evangelical Look at Homosexuality*, (New York: HCCC, 1972), pp. 4-5.
2. I Kings 14:24; II Kings 23:27; Deuteronomy 23:17-18.
3. Martin Noth, *Leviticus: A Commentary* (London: SCM Press, 1965), p. 16; Norman Snaith, *Leviticus and Numbers*, The Century Bible (London: Thomas Nelson, 1967), p. 126.
4. Don Williams, *The Bond That Breaks: Will Homosexuality Split the Church?* (Los Angeles: BIM, 1978), pp. 65, 66.
5. Kenneth Gangel, *The Gospel and the Gay* (Nashville/New York: Thomas Nelson, Inc., 1978), pp. 39-41.
6. Tom Horner, *Jonathan Loved David: Homosexuality in Biblical Times* (Philadelphia: The Westminster Press, 1978), pp. 65-66. Copyright © 1978 Thomas M. Horner. Used by permission of The Westminster Press. This permission also applies to all succeeding passages.
7. John Boswell, *Christianity, Social Tolerance and Homosexuality* (Chicago/London: University of Chicago Press, 1980), p. 100. Used by permission. This permission applies also to all succeeding quotations.
8. See, e.g., Horner, *Jonathan Loved David*, pp. 59-60.
9. I Samuel 18:25-27; Psalm 137:8-9; Psalm 139:19-22 (compare with Matthew 5:43-44).
10. Gangel, *The Gospel and the Gay*, pp. 41-42.
11. Ibid., p. 36.
12. Letha Scanzoni and Virginia Ramey Mollenkott, *Is the Homosexual My Neighbor?* (San Francisco: Harper & Row, 1978), pp. 56-57.
13. Gangel, *The Gospel and the Gay*, p. 69.
14. David Wilkerson, *The Vision*, (Old Tappan, N.J.: Spire Books, Fleming H. Revell Company, 1974), p. 51.
15. Dean Gengle, "An Interview with Revolutionary Psychologist Norman C. Murphy, Ph.D.," *The Advocate* (November 1, 1978), p. 24. Used by permission.

Chapter 6
Law in the Light of Grace

For many readers, the previous chapter on Hebrew perspectives relative to homosexual activities in biblical times would be considered a sufficient analysis of the relevant Old Testament texts on the subject, warranting a dismissal of the levitical Law as having any pertinent bearing upon the gay/God controversy. However, some of the more recent homophobic authors have responded to such an out-of-hand rejection of Mosaic regulations on the part of gay theologians by accusing them of both distortion and deception with regard to their teaching on the inapplicability of the Law for determining the morality of homosexuality. We need, therefore, to examine in more minute detail, the issues regarding the purpose, structure and continuity of the Old Covenant Law through the illumination of New Testament principles.

In the last chapter there was given a concisely as possible review of the Mosaic Law, which laid bare some of its obvious social and moral deficiencies. In this chapter we will study in greater detail some of the faulty fundamentalist logic which inconsistently tries to retain the authority of Old Testament Law (selectively, of course) as a moral precursor for faith and practice.

There are certain basic truths concerning the Law which in the light of Grace need to be forcefully driven home to the reader in this chapter, even at the risk of repetition, if there is ever to be a hope for grounded understanding and practical spiritual comprehension of the issues involved. To say that gays are under Grace requires more than a mere scattering of mushy platitudes about how Jesus loves them as they are in their homosexual orientation. Instead, there needs to be a greater stress on biblical education which can enable more Christians to mentally grasp the essential building blocks which are central to a theology of Grace-in-action relative to sexual expression. But this cannot be done apart from a contrast of the Old with the New, the Law with liberation. To that end this chapter is dedicated.

The place and authority of Old Testament Law has been variously interpreted through the Christian centuries. In this chapter I will not pretend to present an exhaustive overview of the Old Testament legal system, since the theme of this investigation is that of freedom *from* the Law. But it is humorously ironic to find many authors in the ranks of born-again-saved-by-grace religion suddenly retreating behind the stonily lettered walls of a Law-filled theological fortress when all else fails in their attempt to discredit the validity of the gay Christian experience.

The main thrust of their argument is predicated upon the presumption that God's will for our individual moral behavior can be known only through a close examination of the Mosaic revelation of the Law from Sinai—a Law which, according to them, contains in its moral aspects an embodiment of the divine will for, among other things, our sexuality. Seen from the perspective of this line of reasoning, Jesus came not to put an end to the Law, but to reveal it in all its intent, enabling humans to observe its moral tenets through repentant and yielded hearts, rather than through blind obedience impressed upon consciences through rote and tradition. All of this may seem well and good at first impression, but if one is spiritually courageous enough to hack one's way through the jungle of theological camouflage, the stark truth of the teachings of both Jesus and Paul with regard to the nature, purpose, and function of the Law will become readily (and for some, disturbingly) apparent.

One of those evangelical Christians who has been in the forefront of the "gay fray," attacking homosexuality like a modern-day Moses with the Tablets of the Law, is Richard Lovelace, author of *Homosexuality and the Church.* It is Lovelace, with his love for Luther and the Reformed theological tradition, who has placed heavy emphasis on Old Testament Law, especially the Ten Commandments, as being currently applicable in areas dealing with "moral issues." He even goes so far as to reiterate the mistaken assumption of Luther that the true function of the Law is to act in a threefold manner: as the convictor of sin in preparation for conversion and continuing sanctification, as the restrainer of sin, and as the guiding light for ethical conduct.[1] Unfortunately, however, for both Luther and Lovelace, in the Gospel of John, Jesus is recorded as teaching his disciples that what had hitherto been an ongoing function of the Law by virtue of the Mosaic revelation (John 1:17) was now to be supplanted and transferred to the inward ministry of the Holy Spirit. The Spirit is the One who convicts individuals of sin: "And He [the Spirit of truth], when He comes, will convict the world concerning sin, and righteousness, and judgment" (John 16:8 NASV). Furthermore, the responsibility for restraining the world from the extreme proliferation of sin and lawlessness is attributed by most commentators *not* to the Law, but to the supernatural restricting measures of the Holy Spirit and/or the angelic hosts, according to the preordained plan of God's eschatological timetable for the final Apostasy before the long expected return of Christ (II Thessalonians 2:6-8; Revelation 9:1-12).

And as for the contention that the Law is our guidepost for ethical behavior, even well-known fundamentalist M. R. DeHaan has made theological mincemeat of that argument by appealing to the plain and forthright maxims of our Lord, also recorded in the Gospel of John:

> But when He, the Spirit of truth, comes, *He will guide you into all the truth;* for He will not speak on His own initiative, but whatever He hears [from the Father], He will speak; and He will disclose to you what is to come (John 16:13, NASV [emphasis mine]).

It is no wonder, then, that DeHaan emphatically and unequivocally states that *nowhere* in the New Testament is the Law of Moses (which includes the Ten Commandments as well as Leviticus 18:22) said to be a guide for behavior in the life of the Christian.[2] This is not meant to minimize the age-transcending validity of some of the Old Testament precepts. But in Paul's view, Christ had voluntarily taken upon himself the collective penalty due the human race for its continual sin of missing the mark of God's perfect will. In doing so, he fulfilled the Law's demands, leaving us simply the obligation to walk within the morally constraining limits of that God-natured agape love to which the Law itself, in a general-ized way, had always pointed.

> There is therefore now no condemnation for those who are in Christ Jesus. . . . For what the Law could not do, weak as it was through the flesh, God did: sending His own Son in the likeness of sinful flesh and as an offering for sin, He condemned sin in the flesh, in order that the requirement of the Law might be fulfilled in us, who do not walk accord-ing to the flesh, but according to the Spirit.
>
> Owe nothing to anyone except to love one another; *for he who loves his neighbor has fulfilled the law.* For this, "YOU SHALL NOT COMMIT ADULTERY, YOU SHALL NOT MURDER, YOU SHALL NOT STEAL, YOU SHALL NOT COVET," *and if there is any other commandment, it is summed up in this saying,* "YOU SHALL LOVE YOUR NEIGHBOR AS YOURSELF." Love does no wrong to a neighbor; *love therefore is the fulfillment of the law* (Romans 8:1, 3-4; 13:8-10, NASV [emphasis mine]).

The approach of Lovelace and other evangelicals consists of dividing the Law into three parts: the judicial or civil, the ceremo-nial, and the "moral." They contend that the civil precepts of the Mosaic Law are no longer applicable, because God is not at pres-ent reigning through a national culture by virtue of theocratic rule. They further excuse themselves from the necessity of obedience to most of the Levitical dietary and social proscriptions by insisting that these were only ceremonial in nature and devoid of most "moral" significance, having been abolished by Christ. However, when it comes to the Ten Commandments and other aspects of the Law that they hold to be of a "moral" nature, they insist that these commandments—including, of course, the homosexual pro-hibitions found in Leviticus 18:22 and 20:13, are still valid.

When accurately delineated, however, such an approach is at best fanciful and unrealistic. To begin with, when dealing with the issues of Law and Grace from a perceptive biblical perspective, the Old Covenant Law must be considered as a single whole, a mono-lithic unit of commandments. Jesus always referred to it in the singular—"the Law"—not "laws," as if there were separate legal systems which could function independently of one another (Luke 24:44). Paul, also, made it clear that the Law was to be consid-ered as a whole, singular unit:

But before faith came, we were kept under the law [not "laws"], shut up unto the faith which should afterwards be revealed. Wherefore the law [not "laws"] was our schoolmaster to bring us unto Christ, that we might be justified by faith.

But after that faith is come, we are no longer under a schoolmaster [the Law] (Galatians 3:23-25 KJV [emphasis mine]).

Paul's main point in this epistle (which has been coined by some the Magna Carta of Christian liberty from the Law) is that the main function of the Old Testament legal system was to keep the Jewish nation under a strict "tutorial" discipline, until such time as the Messiah would come and offer his people the opportunity to graduate into the maturity of a walk with God by faith. In other words, the Law as a whole has served its purpose in much the same way as the disciplines of elementary and high school. Our graduation diploma became the instrument of our redemption from the grueling routine of classes, homework, and rigid academic requirements. We were set free to walk by faith into the future, having learned to apply the basic principles inherent in our education to situations and circumstances to which *they were applicable*. However, a person beginning a career in professional acting would hardly have use for advanced algebra, which in the past was a requirement. But he or she has now been freed from that mandatory law of schooling; it no longer has a necessary reference to a new life in the freedom of adulthood. According to Paul, it is the same with the Law. And that the Law should be seen as a unified whole can be discerned by taking this analogy a step further: When we graduated from school, we did not graduate from only part of it—we were free from *all* of it. This does not mean that we now ignore all that we learned, for that would be foolish. But it *does* mean that we are free to apply the fruits of our learning *situationally* when they are directly applicable.

That we are free from any obligation to the Law as a contemporary legal discipline is confirmed by no less an authority in fundamentalist circles than Walter Martin.[3] Ironically, the context of Martin's remarks is found in the midst of his attack on Seventh-day Adventist theology, which insists that since the Ten Commandments are eternally valid, it is imperative that we adhere to the literal wording of the Fourth Commandment, which declares that the *seventh day*—not Sunday, the first day of the week—is to be observed as the Sabbath (Exodus 20:8-11). It is at this point in the argument that the Reformed theology of Lovelace and others shows its intrinsic weakness, for they, like the Adventists, insist on the continuing moral applicability of the Ten Commandments.[4] This inconsistency is revealed by their adherence to Sunday observance as fulfilling the requirement of the Fourth Commandment. On this point, however, the Adventists are by far the more theologically consistent in their literal adherence to the biblical text, thereby demonstrating that the followers of Reformed teaching are guilty, according to the Epistle of James, of a sinful transgression: "For whoever keeps the whole Law *and yet stumbles in one point* [in this case, the Fourth Commandment], *he has become guilty of all*" (James 2:10 NASV [emphasis mine]).

With regard to this issue, Robert S. Alley, in his sagaciously controversial *Revolt Against the Faithful*, has correctly observed that many fundamentalist Bible thumpers are hypocritical when they claim to interpret the Scriptures literally, for the seventh day is the only Sabbath known to the Bible![5] It is supremely self-evident that the logic of literalism creates its own limitations. This is clearly the case with Lovelace and his emphasis on the continuing legal validity of Leviticus 18:22, for while holding up the standard of a Mosaic prohibition against homosexual acts (repeated only twice in all of the Old Testament), he and others like him blatantly ignore and habitually violate the third most important commandment in the Hebrew Scriptures (the two others are the Great Commandments exhorting love for God and neighbor [Deuteronomy 6:5; Leviticus 19:18])—that of keeping the Sabbath. Profanation of the Sabbath is threatened with the gravest of spiritual and national consequences in a multitude of scattered biblical pronouncements (Jeremiah 17:19-27; Ezekiel 20:12-26, etc.).

Walter Martin, realizing the problems inherent in recognizing the Ten Commandments as an eternally binding code, has perceptively cut at the very root of such a misconception—the concept of a fragmented Law, part supposedly abolished at the Cross, and part allegedly continuing in force as the Moral Law. This, he says, is nonsense. With passage after passage from Scripture, he convincingly demonstrates, in *Kingdom of the Cults*, the essential unity of the Old Covenant Law. He brings forcibly home the fact that for Paul, the essence of the Law has been distilled into the

Spirit-driven, inward imperative to act and conduct one's life in a way that demonstrates one's love for God and neighbor (Galatians 5:14-23).

Of course, it goes without saying that Walter Martin is probably just as homophobic in his attitude toward the church's acceptance of a gay life-style as are most other theologically conservative Christians, yet the truth of the matter is inescapable: His argument employed against the Seventh-day Adventists and their insistence on Sabbath observance is just as effective as a repudiation of those who decry the acceptance of gay sexuality on the basis of Old Testament Law and its supposed "timeless moral authority." To be sure, the New Testament does counsel us to keep God's commandments (I John 5:2-3), but this should not be construed as a reference to any specific Mosaic precepts. In fact, the First Epistle of John explicitly defines these commandments:

> And whatever we ask we receive from Him, because we keep His commandments and do the things that are pleasing in His sight. *And this is His commandment, that we believe in the name of His Son Jesus Christ, and love one another, just as He commanded us* (I John 3:22-23, NASV [emphasis mine]).

These commandments, then, are simply the maxims of Jesus to believe in God and, correspondingly, to love one another even as Christ has self-sacrificially loved us (Matthew 22:35-40; John 13:1, 34-35). In order to show one's love for the Lord, it is no longer necessary for one to abstain from what were once considered ritually unclean foods, or to continue to observe Saturday as the Sabbath, despite the commands of Leviticus 11; 23:1-3. Taking this logic one step further, when physically expressing one's love for another, it is no longer necessary for the husband to abstain from sexual relations with his wife during her menstrual period, *or for a gay person to refrain from homosexual activity with the person he or she may love, the commandments of Leviticus 20:13, 18 notwithstanding.*

One of the most blatant errors to be found undergirding the argument of Lovelace and others is the assumption that there is a distinction between the "moral law" and the ceremonial and civil ordinances in the Mosaic Covenant. Such theorizing is highly misleading. First, if we assume that the word *moral* refers to that

which is concerned with correct conduct or right principles, the
Old Testament legal system can best be seen as being a "moral
law" in its entirety. It was, in effect, one moral Law, which covered
all the varied aspects of the community's ceremonial, ethical, and
social life. It is important to keep in mind that from a Levitical
perspective, the violation of a ceremonial law was just as much a
moral violation as was a breach of one of the Ten Commandments.
An excellent case in point is the incident recorded in Leviticus
10:1-2, when two priests violated ceremonial precedent and, as a
result, were put to death. To disobey any command that was perceived as having come from God, whether it be ceremonial, dietary, sexual, or ethical, was to commit a moral offense against the
Lord's instructions. It should not be forgotten that the Fall of
humankind described in Genesis 3 was the direct result of the
transgression of a dietary stipulation! So we can see that the
attempt to divorce the various ceremonial and dietary injunctions
of the Law from the "moral" commandments is a thoroughly artificial construct without sound biblical support. The fact that the
Golden Rule (Leviticus 19:18) is situated in the midst of a host of
intermingled ritual, cultic, ceremonial, and sexual regulations,
with no clear-cut division between them, is a pertinent example of
the unified structure of the Law. The Law, therefore, stands or falls
as a single, interrelated body of commandments. If any part of the
Law is still legally and authoritatively binding upon the Christian,
then *all* of it must be perpetually valid, for the Law cannot be
divided into separate, independent systems, but only into various
aspects of the whole. Likewise, if, as Paul insisted, Christ has abolished the Law (Ephesians 2:14-15) in his redemptive work of reconciliation, then *all* the Law has been abolished, both as a means
of attaining righteousness (Romans 10:3-4) and as a final authority
on moral matters (Galatians 5:13-14).

Of course, the usual method of objection against this seemingly
radical Pauline view is an appeal to Matthew 5:17-19, which is in
the heart of the Sermon on the Mount:

> Do not think that I came to abolish the Law or the Prophets;
> I did not come to abolish, but to fulfill. "For truly I say to
> you, until heaven and earth pass away, not the smallest
> letter or stroke shall pass away from the Law, until all is
> accomplished. Whoever then annuls one of the least of
> these commandments, and so teaches others, shall be

called least in the kingdom of heaven; but whoever keeps and teaches them, he shall be called great in the kingdom of heaven" (NASV).

It is usually argued that here, Jesus asserted the Law's perpetually binding nature. But as we have seen, on the basis of the rest of the New Testament teaching (excepting the Epistle of James), such a maxim from our Lord would be seriously at odds with Paul's theology.[6] Furthermore, there are various scholars who question the authenticity of this passage, claiming it to be a later interpolation by Jewish Christians who were opposed to Paul's teaching.[7] Also to be considered is the fact that the tenor of these verses is, for the most part, antithetical to Jesus' general attitude toward the Law as displayed in the other Synoptic Gospels.[8]

To make matters worse, if the statement in verse 19 is interpreted to be in reference to the Mosaic Law mentioned in verses 17-18, then we have a specific instance of our Lord contradicting himself in the same sermon! If verse 19 is a solemn condemnation of any who teach others that even one of the *least* commandments of the Law has been abrogated, then Jesus condemned *himself*, for in the same chapter he goes on to assert the virtual abrogation of the *lex talonis* of Exodus 21:24, to be replaced by his higher call—a call for love that has an ethical regard for human dignity (Matthew 5:38-42). As if that were not enough, he even went so far as to declare as unacceptable the Law's permission for easy divorce (Matthew 5:31-32; Deuteronomy 24:1,3).[9] He also reversed the teaching of the Torah which encouraged the taking of oaths to the Lord (Numbers 30:2; Matthew 5:33-37). This obviously creates many serious difficulties for the literalist who takes Matthew 5:19 at face value, since it serves as a condemnation of Pauline theology and encourages Christ's followers to continue in the Judaic religious tradition that has always highly exalted the Law.[10]

Evangelicals who use the passage as a justification for their argument that gays must not ignore the homosexual condemnations of the Old Testament levitical precepts cannot have it both ways. They cannot appeal to the Apostle Paul for scriptural support of their refusal to observe portions of the Law to which they object, yet run for refuge to the purported sayings of Jesus which seemingly uphold the entire Law's everlasting validity!

There is basically only one way the words of Matthew 5:17-19 can be interpreted so as not to conflict with Paul's concept of Law in relation to Grace, and even then the interpretation is risky, in that it does not have overwhelming support among biblical scholars. I personally doubt the authenticity of these verses, but if we were to assume them to be genuine, at the same time maintaining that Jesus did *not* in the same chapter contradict his own words, then we have little leeway for any acceptable exegesis other than the following.

Verse 17 is a declaration by Jesus to the effect that he came as the messianic fulfillment of all for which the Law stood, and toward which the prophets had pointed. Many of the actions and sayings of Christ as recorded in the Gospels were taken by the rank and file of the people and priests as an indication that he was advocating a disrespect and disregard for the Law. Therefore, in this verse Jesus was seeking to clarify this misconception by claiming that he had not come to destroy the significance of the Law, but to fill to the fullest extent all that it pointed toward, through his ministry of love and reconciliation. But in verse 18 he pointedly emphasized that the Law would remain in force "*until* all is accomplished." If we interpret this to be an eschatological reference to the final consummation of all things (I Corinthians 15:28), we are once again faced with a statement incompatible with other recorded remarks of Jesus himself, as well as the later writings of Paul. Here we must ask, What did Jesus consider to be this "final accomplishment"? The most satisfying answer would seem to be found in his last cry uttered from the Cross before committing his spirit into the safekeeping of God: "It is accomplished" (John 19:30). In other words, the purpose of his ministry had been fulfilled; his life had served as the preeminent example of One who had lived to love and had died to prove its eternal efficaciousness, thus summing up all that the ancient written code of the Mosaic legacy had, at best, only feebly foreshadowed. The Law had continued for centuries among the Israelites in its ordained function as the instrument of the sinner's condemnation for transgression and served them as a daily reminder of their own human imperfection (II Corinthians 3:1-11). But the era of the Law was passing away (Hebrews 8:13). At Calvary, it was Love that triumphed over Law. In his capacity of Messiah, Jesus cancelled the condemnatory role of Israel's Law through his redemptive death (Romans 8:1; Colossians 2:14-16).

Throughout the Sermon on the Mount, we see Jesus reiterating his respect for the Law within the context of its divinely ordained purpose, but at the same time, he was preparing his disciples for the eventual realization of its obsolescence. Christ knew that the Law would soon come to its appointed end in the purpose of God's redemptive economy, culminating in that final sacrificial act of messianic servanthood, the Cross.

When Jesus warned against abrogating "the least of these commandments," he must have been referring (if the saying is indeed genuine), not to the ordinances of the Law, but to the commandments he was about to give, some of which actually contradicted the letter of the Mosaic Law. Jesus was introducing a higher Kingdom ethic, which he intended to remain in the practice of his disciples long after the Law had come to an end through the redemptive fulfillment.

Jesus' attitude toward the Law was certainly one of immense respect (Mark 7:9-13), but it never seemed to reach the proportions of exaggerated reverence common to the traditional Jewish piety of his time. There are some scholars who are confident that what was later formulated by Paul as a developed theology, proclaiming freedom from the legalism and bondage engendered by the reign of the Law of Moses over Jewish life, actually can be traced back to the subtle, antinomian strains which irregularly laced their way through the substructure of Jesus' teaching.[11]

All too often, orthodox Christian theologians have desperately attempted to evade the full force of some of the bluntly confrontative statements uttered by our Lord against those religious leaders who were known for their strict adherence to the letter of the Law, but who ignored its spirit. When examined without the aid of the stained-glass spectacles of religious wishful thinking, there emerges from the Gospel pages a disturbing picture of a radical rabbi from Nazareth, whose fiercely independent teachings did not hesitate to set aside the demanding requirements of the Law when he perceived them as obstacles to the fulfillment of human needs. As much as Jerry Falwell, Tim LaHaye, and others in the ranks of the New Right religionists thrive on their volatile tirades against the "lurking monster of humanism," it is plainly evident that Jesus Christ stands foremost among the historic, prophetic figures of the world's faiths as a Teacher par excellence of inspired *religious* humanism.[12]

Jesus did not need to resort to the Law for justification of his views; he was his own authority! He supported and made reference to the tenets of the Law when they were instrumental in reinforcing some portion of his teaching. However, at other times, his flagrant violation of the Law was a source of scandal to the Pharisees. A prime example is found in the Gospel of Mark:

> And it came about that [Jesus] was passing through the grainfields on the Sabbath, and His disciples began to make their way along while picking the heads of grain. And the Pharisees were saying to Him, "See here, why are they doing what is not lawful on the Sabbath?" And He said to them, "Have you never read what David did when he was in need and became hungry, he and his companions: how he entered the house of God in the time of Abiathar the high priest, and ate the consecrated bread, which is not lawful for anyone to eat except the priests, and he gave it also to those who were with him?" And He was saying to them, "The Sabbath was made for man, and not man for the Sabbath. Consequently, the Son of Man is Lord even of the Sabbath" (Mark 2:23-28 NASV).

In this controversial incident, several things become significant. The Jews pointedly accused him of breaking the Sabbath law. And *Jesus never denied the accusation.* Christ clearly perceived himself as technically violating the Law, for as we have just read, his defense was the recounting of a situation mentioned in the sacred writings, when David, one of the greatest prophet-kings of Israel, also broke the Law and—from Jesus' standpoint—*with justification* (Leviticus 24:5-9; I Samuel 21:1-6). Again, a basic human need was at issue: hunger. For Jesus, as a religious humanist, the solution was simple: Human need takes precedent over the Law. Therefore, breaking the Law is not always sinful; sometimes it can accomplish the highest good. We see here also the beginning of a tendency toward a modified form of situational ethics, which regarded the Mosaic commandments as helpful moral guidelines only so far as they were applicable as the morally superior and practically relevant solution to any given circumstance. This, as Jesus knew, most definitely could not be said for the entire Law.

Gospel passages such as that taken from Mark often prove to be very embarrassing to numerous Christians of orthodox persuasion, for it shows that our Lord at times was a willful lawbreaker.

This causes complications, especially among evangelicals who insist that Jesus kept the Law perfectly and was without sin. The fallacy of this is that one assumption is not contingent upon the other. Jesus was without sin (Hebrews 4:15)—not because he obeyed every commandment in the Torah, but because he followed the will of God for his life, part of which was to point people *beyond* the rigid strictures intrinsic to the letter of the Law.

Christ's teaching with regard to the transiency of the Mosaic dispensation is further developed farther along in Mark's Gospel. Conversing with his disciples after another confrontation with his religious opponents, Jesus went on the declare:

> "Are you so lacking in understanding also? Do you not understand that whatever goes into the man from outside cannot defile him; because it does not go into his heart, but into his stomach, and is eliminated?" (Thus He declared all foods clean). (Mark 7:18-19 NASV).

It should be noted that the sentence within the parentheses is an editorial comment by the author John Mark (probably at the instruction of the apostle Peter, since it is widely believed that Mark was writing, to a large extent, the memoirs of Peter). Clearly, the apostolic author was quick to point out to his predominantly Gentile audience that Jesus' remarks were specifically aimed at paving the way for the demise of the Law. In this passage from the Gospels we find the dietary regulations of the Old Testament (Leviticus 11; Deuteronomy 14) coming under the scrutinizing judgment of One who was a greater prophet than Moses (Deuteronomy 18:18). The result was the prefiguring of a reversal within the heart of the Mosaic legal framework. What Moses had proclaimed to Israel as being ritually unclean for dietary consumption, the Messiah majestically reversed by a casual observation about what actually constitutes true defilement (Mark 7:14-23). Obviously, the disciples did not grasp the stunning significance of Christ's words at the time; only in retrospect could their full import be discerned.[13] This underscores the earlier mention of the *subtle* antinomianism that pervades the "higher mysteries" (Mark 4:11-12) of our Lord's teachings. Jesus was laying the foundations of transition from one spiritual dispensation to another through his interpretive analysis of the past Mosaic tradition. He instinctively extracted the highest moral principles and integrated them into his own vision of Kingdom living, while leaving the dross of archaic, culturally superfluous, or ethically undesirable commandments of the Law to their fate of approaching impotence.

When studied in the shadow of Christ's preceding ministry, Paul's conclusions concerning the nature, goal, and fulfillment of the Mosaic legislation are not surprising, based in large part as they are upon the kernels of forgiving and redemptive grace found scattered throughout the soil of the Master's instructions pertaining to the will of God and the living of an abundant life. Jesus had only hinted at his liberal views regarding the Law in occasional challenging remarks addressed to his religious detractors or to his own disciples. But Paul felt persuaded by the Spirit that it was the appointed time in God's plan for the divine "secret" to be revealed: a sacred mystery which involved the union of Jew and Gentile into one redeemed, spiritual body of people, a union made possible only by the removal of the barrier that had caused Israel's ethnic separation from the nations—the Law (Ephesians 2:13-16; 3:1-6).

The apostle, like Jesus, had great respect for the Law when seen in its religiohistorical context, as a tool by which God could make the Jews acutely aware of their own sinful nature, so that it was impossible to live up to the highest moral expectations of the divine will without the forgiveness and enabling grace of the Messiah's redemption (Romans 3:31; 7). And, according to Paul's Epistles, the saving act of Christ on the Cross did precisely that. We have been transferred into the Kingdom of the Son (Colossians 1:13), who rules his people not by the Law, but by Love. "But now we have been released from the Law, having died to that by which we were bound, so that we serve in newness of the Spirit and not in oldness of the letter" (Romans 7:6 NASV).

When we examine the writings of Paul closely, it is easy to see that in certain aspects of his doctrinal formulation, he was distinctively antinomian in his approach to the Law of the Old Testament.[14] He denied that the Law was a means of attaining righteousness (Romans 10:4), or that it could dictate a way of life for the Christian (Galatians 4:21–5:14). This is why Paul reiterated in his Epistle to the Corinthians, "*All things are lawful*, but not all things are profitable. *All things are lawful*, but not all things edify" (I Corinthians 10:23 NASV [emphasis mine]). All things are "lawful" for Christians, because we are not under the Law, which alone can technically declare our actions "illegal" or "unlawful." To put it in the most blatant terms, as a Christian, one theoretically can steal, commit adultery, or even murder, and the act would be considered "lawful," since the church is not under the legal jurisdiction of the Law (Romans 6:14). *However,* to engage in such immoral violations of love toward neighbor would definitely not, as Paul said, be profitable or edifying; in fact, it would make one ineligible to enter the final, eschatological realization of the kingdom of God (Galatians 5:19-21). For Paul, it was never a question of what is lawful, since the Mosaic Law has no place as an instrument of Christian regulation. It will, rather, always be a question of what is or is not a departure from the fruits of gracious behavior and attitude which characterize a walk with God in the Spirit. For this reason, Paul continued to write in the Corinthian epistle, "Let no one seek his own good, but that of his neighbor" (I Corinthians 10:24 NASV). This brings us to the heart and spirit of the matter: Love of neighbor and love of God is the final common denominator by which the individual Christian is to determine the appropriateness or desirability of any specific conduct.

In I Corinthians 6:12, Paul uses the same statement ("All things are lawful") when discussing the issue of sexual immorality (in this case, prostitution). It is extremely illuminating that Paul does not appeal to any part of the Law, including the Seventh Commandment, to prove his point. Instead, he resorts to the utilization of reason and common sense, probably because of his understanding that an appeal to the Law as being legally relevant would be contrary to his gospel message. But in appealing to the spiritual faculties of reason and discernment, he was encouraging the people to *think for themselves* concerning morality, based upon the counsel of God's love shed abroad within their hearts by the Holy Spirit (Romans 5:5; 14:22; Colossians 1:9-10).

To perceive a moral truth, it is not necessary for us to run to the Law for definition, any more than we would return to elementary school to learn the solution to a complicated problem of calculus or trigonometry. It is the Holy Spirit who guides and instructs us deep within the "inner knowing" of the human spirit. Christians need to leave their preoccupation with the Law behind them and learn to go forward to discover a religious and moral maturity which can be developed only by an increasing ability to discern the Spirit's whispers of direction to the searching soul. The Spirit is not chained to either the Law or traditions entrenched within the Hebrew Scriptures; the Spirit is free and unbound like the wind (John 3:8). It murmurs the secrets of priceless truth on the gentle breezes of inspiration and enlightenment, which may be activated by a myriad of different sources. But one *knows* when the Spirit has spoken; one need not constantly consult the written inspiration of the past, valuable though it may be, in order to discern the truth of God's contemporaneous communion with the human spirit.

David Field, in his treatise opposing homosexual acceptance in the church—*The Homosexual Way—A Christian Option?*—places great emphasis upon I Timothy 1:8-11 as a description of the place of the Law, especially the Decalogue, in the Christian's life.[15] Claiming that these verses are actually an informal listing of violations of the Ten Commandments, arranged in the same general order as the Commandments themselves, he goes on to insist that Paul loosely categorizes the *arsenokoitai* (translated variously as *sodomites* or *homosexuals*) mentioned in verse 10 as being in violation of the Seventh Commandment, therefore proving that homosexual activity is a violation of God's "moral law." As will be shown in chapter 7, lexicographical investigation of *arsenokoitai* has more than convincingly concluded that its meaning in the mind and culture of the Apostle Paul was that of male prostitutes, not homosexuals in general. The body of historical evidence supports the contention that male as well as female prostitutes were often frequented by married men in Hellenistic society. This would therefore account for the association of the *arsenokoitai* as being the means by which these married men occasionally consummated their adultery. First Timothy 1:10 does not prove that all homosexual activity is necessarily to be equated with acts of adultery. Such a viewpoint is a thoroughly unwarranted assumption, based on nothing more than an overly extended interpretation of the Seventh Commandment.

Even more disconcerting, with regard to Field's endeavor to incorporate this passage from chapter 1 of I Timothy into his arsenal of proof texts for the continuing validity of the Law, is the self-evident fact that verses 3-7, Paul's preface to verses 8-11, contain an indictment upon certain teachers in the churches under Timothy's jurisdiction who had set themselves up as "doctors of the Law" and placed great emphasis upon it in their arguments.

They were evidently Judaistic in their doctrinal slant, hence their accentuation of the Old Testament's centrality to the new fledgling faith, even down to the most minute of speculative trivia relating to the patriarchal genealogies. Paul would have none of this, and he told Timothy to enforce his clerical authority against them. The great apostle explained his primary reason for concern: "The only purpose of this instruction is that there should be love, coming out of a pure heart, a clear conscience and a sincere faith" (I Timothy 1:5 JB). Obviously, these heretical teachers were placing extra burdens of condemnation upon the consciences of the faithful, demanding that Spirit-directed love alone could not suffice for a Christian's sense of moral direction if it lacked the Law to give it explanatory definition. This is what Paul opposed, just as he opposed it in the congregations throughout Galatia. In verses 8-9, he proceeds to explain the fatal theological flaw: "We know, of course, that the Law is good, but only provided it is treated like any law, *in the understanding that laws are not framed for people who are good*" (JB [emphasis mine]). His subsequent listing of various transgressions of the Law's commands was done for precisely the *opposite* reason from that put forth by most anti-gay expositors. Paul was not setting down the Law *as law* for the Christian, since he had just stated that laws were not made for the righteous. Christians, having been made righteous by divine fiat through the redemptive work of Christ *apart* from the Law (Romans 3:28), have no need for codified laws, since their behavioral response to God and neighbor is motivated by the love of Jesus welling up within their souls (Galatians 5:23).

Arguing as I do against the establishment of any vestiges of levitical legalism in the imperatives for a Christian life is not meant to imply that none of the old Mosaic regulations are without intrinsic moral value. Quite the contrary, many of the Old Covenant's commandments are repeatedly found scattered throughout the pages of the New Testament, though never in the sense of a new law. They were, instead, reiterated because they derived their moral worth from their timeless applicability. Such can be said for most of the Ten Commandments, yet the repetition of these dictums in the early Christian Scriptures was always for the purpose of upholding their ongoing moral viability, completely divorced from any dependence on the Jewish legal system in which they had previously been contained. The only "law" ever depicted in the New Testament is the "law of Christ" (I Corinthians 9:21). And what is the law of Christ? The imperative to *love*:

> A new commandment I give to you, that you love one another, even as I have loved you, that you also love one another. "By this all men will know that you are My disciples, if you have love for one another."
>
> Bear one another's burdens, and thus fulfill the law of Christ (John 13:34-35; Galatians 6:2 NASV).

In the final analysis, the issue of homosexuality's appropriateness of expression within the context of a Christian life-style cannot properly be determined by reference to the ordinances of Mosaic Law. How, then, is a devout believer able to discriminate between right behavior which honors God, and wrongful conduct, which dishonors the Lord and morally degrades the individual? One of the best general yardsticks given in the New Testament is found in Paul's Epistle to the Galatians:

> But if you are led by the Spirit, you are not under the Law. Now the deeds of the flesh are evident, which are: immorality, impurity, sensuality, idolatry, sorcery, enmities, strife, jealousy, outbursts of anger, disputes, dissensions, factions, envying, drunkenness, carousing, and things like these, of which I forewarn you ... that those who practice such things shall not inherit the kingdom of God. But the fruit of the Spirit is love, joy, peace, patience, kindness, goodness, faithfulness, gentleness, self-control; against such things there is no law (Galatians 5:18-23 NASV).

In light of verse 19, with its threefold condemnation of immorality (*porneia* [Gk.]—prostitution), sexual impurity, and illicit sensuality, it can be justifiably asserted that a committed homosexual relationship which avoids the pitfalls of adultery, prostitution, promiscuity, and lustful, erotic obsession is a holy union worthy of the sanctification of Jesus Christ. It is therefore perfectly legitimate to conclude that as long as gay Christians allow themselves to be led by the Spirit, harvesting in their daily lives the fruits that regeneratively issue forth from a spiritual commitment to God, to that extent, they have fulfilled the love-expectations of the New Testament for personal holiness and moral respectability.

NOTES

1. Richard Lovelace, *Homosexuality and the Church* (Old Tappan, N.J.: Fleming H. Revell Co., 1978), p. 76.

2. M. R. DeHaan, *Law or Grace* (Grand Rapids: Zondervan Publishing House, 1965), pp. 140-41.

3. Walter Martin, *The Kingdom of the Cults* (Minneapolis: Bethany Fellowship Publishers, 1965, 1977), pp. 412-19.

4. Lovelace, *Homosexuality and the Church*, pp. 81, 89-90.

5. Robert S. Alley, *Revolt Against the Faithful: A Biblical Case for Inspiration as Encounter* (Philadelphia/New York: J. B. Lippincott Co., 1970), pp. 92-93.

6. Probably no other part of the New Testament has undergone more meticulous scrutiny in an awkward attempt to reconcile the obvious differences between Paul and James, relative to the function and place of the Law and good works, than the Epistle of James itself. While most evangelicals are solidly committed to an approach that spares no amount of theological gymnastics in order to harmonize the two apostles' conflicting viewpoints, I personally find it much more intellectually satisfying to accept their differences at face value, as an example of the kind of heated religious debate ongoing among the factions within the early church. Despite the reams of doctrinal dissertations which declare that there is really an underlying agreement between Paul and James if one correctly understands the scriptural contexts, certain glaring contradictions still stand out like sore thumbs of theology unable to be healed. For example, in Paul's mind the Law was an instrument of death and condemnation (II Corinthians 3:7-9), but to James it was the perfect Law of liberty (James 2:8-12). For Paul, liberty was life in the Spirit, free of the Law's bondage (II Corinthians 3:17; Galatians 5:1-5). It was the party of James in Jerusalem that was not only zealous for the Law, but was even influential enough to cause Peter to draw back from openly siding with Paul at Antioch on the whole issue of the Law being superceded by the grace and reconciliation of Christ (Acts 21:20; Galatians 2:11-12). It would seem that James' Epistle is a reaction to Paul's teaching as expounded in Romans 3 & 4 (or at least to a version of it which he may have heard second-hand), for while Paul utilizes Abraham as an example of salvation by faith alone, James replies by using the same Hebrew patriarch as an example of good works as a prerequisite for the validation of faith as a saving vehicle in redemption. Whether James was directly addressing Paul's moderately antinomian views concerning the Law, or was reacting to a misunderstanding of the apostle's teachings, is not certain; but the distinct Jewish imprint of the Law's centrality pervades the thinking of James, unlike that of either Paul or Jesus.

7. J. C. Fenton, *Saint Matthew* (Philadelphia: The Westminster Press, 1963), p. 85.

8. See e.g., Luke 13:15-16; 14:1-6.

9. It is extremely amusing to observe the obvious inconsistencies of many fundamentalists who, while pompously proclaiming their unswerving allegiance to the principles of biblical literalism, nevertheless find it necessary to strain at gnats and swallow camels in a last-ditch effort to find some way to avoid the literal meaning of Jesus' seemingly uncompromising stance on divorce and remarriage. It would seem that conservative Christians are much more liberal in their scriptural exegesis when it involves an issue that affects a significant number within their own congregations. They know only too well the disastrous social and financial effects that could devastate their churches if they applied the words of Jesus literally by forbidding the remarriage of all those who have divorced on any grounds other than adultery, and by threatening excommunication to all who do remarry. But to apply the same kind of spiritual magnanimity to

homosexuals? "God forbid!" they say. "That would be tampering with the Word of God!" At any rate, "consistency thou art a jewel" is certainly not a slogan that accurately reflects fundamentalist and evangelical theology, as their varying range of positions on divorce definitely demonstrate.

10. A similar passage of doubtful origin is found in Matthew 23:2-3, where Jesus is recorded as commanding his disciples to observe and obey all that the scribes and Pharisees teach (despite their personal hypocrisy), for they "sit in the seat of Moses." If the disciples had followed such advice literally, the Church never would have been formed as distinct from Judaism, and we would still be attending synagogue on the Sabbath in order to carefully ascertain the teaching and traditions of the elders! It is hard to believe such a statement could have been uttered by our Lord, in light of his oft recorded attacks upon many of the Pharisees' specific teachings (Matthew 15:3-14, etc.). See also J. C. Fenton, *Saint Matthew*, p. 366.

11. Morton Smith, *The Secret Gospel: The Discovery and Interpretation of the Secret Gospel According to Mark* (New York/San Francisco: Harper & Row, 1973), pp. 111-14, 133ff.

12. For the sake of clarification, a distinction between secular humanism and Christian humanism is in order. Secular humanism is antisupernaturalistic in its philosophical inclinations, positing humankind at the center of the moral universe as the ultimate arbiter of its own destiny. Christian humanism, on the other hand, has God as its primary focus, Deity being the omipotent Mind-force which, through revelation, gives ultimate value and moral meaning to human existence. It is because "God so loved the world" (John 3:16) that Jesus strove to demonstrate God's concern for the human race through teachings and actions which exemplified the sterling worth of individuals made in the image of the God who loves them. That loving God, who sent forth the Son into the world to redeem, showed in Jesus Christ the Godhead's humanistic concentration upon the fulfillment of the human potential which the race had been created to achieve.

13. Charles Gore, ed., *A New Commentary on Holy Scripture* (New York: the MacMillan Company, 1928), pp. 74-75.

14. A distinction needs to be made between the moderate antinomianism of Paul, solely with regard to the Mosaic legal system's claim on the life-style of a Christian, and the *extreme* antinomianism characteristic of the Gnostic libertines who maintained that they were free from obligation to *any* set of moral principles. This heresy the apostle vigorously opposed throughout his epistles.

15. David Field, *The Homosexual Way—A Christian Option?* (Downers Grove, Ill.: InterVarsity Press, Revised ed. © 1979 by David Field. Used by permission of InterVarsity Press, Downers Grove, IL 60515. 1979), pp. 31-32.

Chapter 7
Paul on Perversion

When we come to the pages of the New Testament, it is the first chapter of Paul's Epistle to the Romans that is, without a doubt, used most often as a damning indictment against homosexuality. We should, therefore, begin by examining this disputed passage in specific detail.

> For the wrath of God is revealed from heaven against all ungodliness and unrighteousness of men, who suppress the truth in unrighteousness, because that which is known about God is evident within them; for God made it evident to them. For since the creation of the world His invisible attributes, His eternal power and divine nature, have been clearly seen, being understood through what has been made, so that they are without excuse. For even though they knew God, they did not honor Him as God, or give thanks; but they became futile in their speculations, and their foolish heart was darkened. Professing to be wise, they became fools, and exchanged the glory of the incorruptible God for an image in the form of corruptible man and of birds and four-footed animals and crawling creatures.
>
> Therefore God gave them over in the lusts of their hearts to impurity, that their bodies might be dishonored among them. For they exchanged the truth of God for a lie, and worshiped and served the creature rather than the Creator, who is blessed forever. Amen.
>
> For this reason God gave them over to degrading pas-

sions; for their women exchanged the natural function for that which is unnatural, and in the same way also the men abandoned the natural function of the woman and burned in their desire toward one another, men with men committing indecent acts and receiving in their own persons the due penalty of their error (Romans 1:18-27 NASV).

One of the most serious flaws found in expositions of Romans 1 is the assumption that all homosexual activity is a manifestation of sexual *perversion*. This approach fails to take into account the very real and verifiable distinction in modern psychology between sexual *per*version and sexual *in*version. *Perversion* involves a conscious choice to take part in sexual activity that is opposed to the person's natural instincts. It is usually associated with psychological abnormality, and in the view of Scripture, is an indication of the deepest individual and societal corruption. *Inversion*, on the other hand, is the sexual orientation one discovers in oneself, quite apart from any conscious choice. It is a basic, integrated aspect of a person's total selfhood and sense of identity, which, while its cause and origin are not always explainable, is nevertheless a reality that will not go away; and despite all attempts, it has not been proved to be reversible. It is evident from even a cursory reading of Romans 1 that the deviation Paul had in mind was definitely sexual perversion. In fact, it is highly doubtful that Paul was even aware of the realities of sexual inversion. It is plain from this excerpt that he was predicating his argument upon the *assumption* that the persons he described were, in fact, practicing heterosexuals who, because of their rebellious and idolatrous state, had "given up" relations with the opposite sex. It should be added here that there are some gay Christian apologists who have argued that Paul was intentionally exempting homosexual inverts from his stinging condemnation, since he mentioned only heterosexuals who participate in same-sex activity, but this is creating a hypothetical distinction in the mind of Paul. Certainly he would have made reference to and exemption for the difference between perversion and inversion, had he really been aware of it. We have no right to interpret Paul's Epistles in any way that would be inconsistent with his contemporary cultural, social, and theological assumptions. In other words, since it is almost certain that Paul, like most people of his day, considered everyone to have been created naturally heterosexual, we are bound to interpret his words in Romans as being a rejection of *all* homosexual activity as perversion, since it deviated from the God-ordained norm of heterosexuality. This is the most logical and consistent interpretation of Paul's statements. However, we are certainly not under obligation to believe that Paul's outlook on this subject was free from judgmental error, even though fundamentalists claim that the Holy Spirit somehow preserved all the biblical writers from any degree of fallibility.

If we were bound by all the scientific and sociological concepts of the biblical authors, we would indeed be in a pickle. Some commonly held opinions of their day will make this point clear. Many of the ancients subscribed to the view that the earth was flat and supported by pillars. They were also believers in the primitive system of astronomy which postulated that the earth was the center of the universe, with the sun and planets revolving around it. In the sociological sphere, many of their practices would be revolting to our innate sense of humanitarianism. Slavery was an accepted practice; women were considered to be the rightful property of men. The list could go on and on. These belief-systems and cultural practices eventually proved to be either in error or unacceptable by later moral standards. There is no logical reason for us to abide by many of those ancient concepts; they are only an indication of the limited perspective commonly shared by the authors of Scripture in their social environment and culture.

While it is fairly certain that Paul had negative opinions concerning homosexual acts, it is essential to realize that the twentieth-century believer is not bound by the apostle's private or penned opinions, but by the basic principles he gave us—principles that can be relevantly related to the sociological/cultural situation confronting us in this current sexual controversy. The probable fact that Paul was not aware of inversion as a psychological reality within the context of sexuality does not invalidate its right to a fair and objective examination as a category quite separate from the perversion of which the apostle spoke in Romans 1. The words of Paul in this controversial passage clearly were based upon an assumption that all the persons to whom he made reference were practicing heterosexuals, leaving ("exchanging") their normal inclinations for a depraved life-style of hedonistic abandonment.

Qualified commentators agree that, for the most part, the Bible is not dealing with confirmed homosexuals. The biblical judgments came against a background of moral decadence in which all of life had come loose at the seams, and people experimented wildly with just about every form of sexual activity. When Paul says that homosexual behavior runs against nature, he is talking about a heterosexual person who, against his basic inclinations, engages in homosexual activity. The man he is talking about is not, at the core, a homosexual person. . . .

Why the Bible makes no distinction between heterosexual people who engage in homosexual acts and confirmed homosexual people is easily understood. The confirmed homosexual was not recognized until roughly 1890. The Bible writers assumed that everyone was heterosexual and that in times of moral decay, some heterosexual people did some strange and unnatural things with each other.[1]

The wording of the scriptural passage is therefore very important, for such terminology as "exchanged" and "given up" cannot be applied to confirmed homosexual inverts, since most of them never had any vestiges of heterosexual practices to give up in the first place! To use Romans 1:18-27 as a judgmental sword against homosexual inverts who are definitely not attracted to the opposite sex and who, for the most part, have never been involved in sexual relations with them, amounts to stretching the apostle's words far beyond their original intent—that acting contrary to natural instincts is yet another indication of humanity's fallen and alienated state of confusion. Such a principle can similarly be applied, in light of present psychological knowledge, to the situation of gays in the present predominately heterosexual society, which seeks to force them into molds and relations that are contrary to their nature. If homosexuals allow themselves to be drawn into a denial of their inner sexual instincts out of an idolatrous regard for the orientation of the majority, they would be committing the same kind of sinful folly as that described by Paul in Romans 1 with respect to heterosexuals.

In a publication titled *The Homosexual Way—A Christian Option?* David Field argues that

in Romans 1, the theological context is *creation*. . . .

In writing about "natural relations," Paul is not referring to individual men and women *as they are*. His canvas is much broader. He is taking the argument back, far more radically, to man and woman *as God created them*. By "unnatural" he means "unnatural to mankind in God's creation pattern." And that pattern he clearly understands to be heterosexual. . . . The "exchange" he has in mind is not just the capricious sex swapping of the pervert in his search for fresh stimulation, but the divergence *all* homosexual behavior represents from God's creation scheme. When set in the context of creation, all homosexual relations are "unnatural relations." [2]

On the surface, this argument seems formidable, but upon closer scrutiny and a careful rereading of Romans 1, one can detect numerous flaws in this approach. First, theologically, this passage centers on the conflict between the truth of God's transcendent Deity and the degrading Lie of idolatry (v. 25). The subject of creation is utilized only as a form of testimony to the Truth (vs. 19-20). David Field's sweeping assertion that "when set in the context of creation, all homosexual relations are 'unnatural' " is defied by the observations of modern primate behavioral studies, which validate the *manifest truth* of the present created order:

The data on homosexual behavior among infrahuman mammals indicate that it occurs among the lowest as well as among the highest mammals, but that as we ascend the phylogenetic scale both the frequency and the complexity of this behavior increase; among the subhuman primates we get a clear inference of the type of homosexuality that exists at the level of human life. . . .

On the basis of the phylogenetic data, and on the basis of the cross-cultural data . . . it is not too rash to assume, as West did, that "Homosexual behavior seems to arise from some *deep-rooted natural urge* which finds different expression in different cultures." . . .

No sexual behavior, whether heterosexual, homosexual, or autoerotic in character, is without a firm foundation in phylogeny and developmental history of the species (emphasis mine).[3]

From this we can only conclude that, quite contrary to Field's opinion, homosexuality is a legitimate variant form of sexual expression and that it is sanctioned by nature. The accusation that any genital expressions of gay sexuality are unnatural is based, not upon biological or anthropological evidence (which contradict such an assertion), but to a large degree upon certain Greek words in Romans 1:26, translated variously as "unnatural" and "against nature." Authors of recent articles and books dealing with the theological aspects of homosexuality have predictably lined up on one side or the other, depending upon their presuppositions concerning the moral acceptability of the gay life-style. Evangelical authors like LaHaye, Lovelace, Gangel, and Williams merely take Paul's words at face value, claiming that this is the obvious meaning of the text. They further insinuate that pro-gay religious defenders are "trying to pull rabbits out of hats" by what they consider flimsy arguments aimed at avoiding the full condemnatory force of the term "against nature." To some extent, they may be correct, in that whatever the actual meaning of the Greek words, nothing can mitigate the fact that they are definitely opprobrious in their context, despite the fine variations of meaning that could be applied.

However, other Christian writers such as Scanzoni and Mollenkott, Boswell, and McNeill are not satisfied that the case is so cut and dried. McNeill has suggested that the words could be interpreted to mean a violation, not of natural biological urges, but of customary attitudes, the virtuous mores of respectable Gentile society, or perhaps the levitical customs of Jewish Law.[4] John Boswell of Yale University has written by far the most detailed analysis of the words in question, and he concludes that

> for Paul, "nature" was not a question of universal law or truth but, rather a matter of the *character* of some person or group of persons, a character which was largely ethnic and entirely human: Jews are Jews "by nature," just as Gentiles are Gentiles "by nature." ...
>
> It is not "nature" in the abstract but *someone's* nature. ...
>
> "Nature" in Romans 1:26, then, should be understood as the *personal* nature of the pagans in question. ...
>
> Paul believed that the Gentiles knew of the truth of God

but rejected it and likewise rejected their true "nature" as regarded their sexual appetites, going beyond what was "natural" for them and what was approved for the Jews.[5]

This too, is an extremely plausible explanation, which necessarily punctures Field's statement that Paul could have been referring only to the universal behavioral laws of nature.

Yet there is no need to be so picky about the meaning of these words, when one realizes that there is not one shred of evidence that Paul ever conceived of a legitimate and divinely acceptable expression of homosexual behavior. The more fellow gay theologians continue to press the argument that Paul was only castigating certain kinds of homosexual acts (giving the impression that *other* kinds might be OK), the more they will lose their credibility as unbiased students and interpreters of the Scriptures, gaining instead a reputation for theological sophistry.

Again, it must be emphasized that everything the apostle stated in Romans 1 was based upon the mistaken assumption that the human race was created exclusively heterosexual. The book of Leviticus had left no room for homosexual "exceptions," and it is clear from the verses Paul penned to the Roman Christians that, at that point in his understanding, he had not been enlightened by any revelation to the contrary. Just as we see Paul vacillating between his revelation of women's equality in Christ (Galatians 3:28) and the deeply ingrained sexist attitudes originating from his Orthodox Jewish background (I Timothy 2:9-15), so it also stands to reason that it would have been remarkable for him to have had such an open attitude toward a form of sexuality that was abhorred in Judaism. So it becomes increasingly clear that whether Paul (like Field) mistakenly believed that homosexual expressions were deviations from the natural created order, or simply a violation of decent community standards, it amounts to the same thing: Paul believed homosexual behavior to be outside the will of God. Sadly, I must say that on these points I find myself in agreement with Jerry R. Kirk, an anti-gay Presbyterian minister and author:

> Some homosexual apologists, such as Bailey and McNeill, have tried to sidestep this passage [Romans 1] by asserting that Paul was castigating homosexual lust and promiscuity rather than homosexual acts. . . .

Romans and Greeks had long rationalized homosexuality, and even Plato in the *Symposium* gave it his approval. It
is unthinkable that Paul would not designate which kinds
of homosexual behavior he would approve, especially given
the place it occupies in his thesis regarding the fall of man
in the first chapter of Romans. He certainly drew distinc-
tions when it came to other ethical questions. He drew
lines between sufficient and insufficient grounds for divorce. He differentiated between a proper and an improper
use of meat offered to idols. He contrasted constructive
exhortation with judgmental rebuke. He discriminated between good and bad use of the law.

But here, with this major issue, Paul made no distinc-
tions. Both homosexual lust *and* behavior were categori-
cally rejected and condemned as sinful. The *acts* were
condemned.[6]

In some Christian literary quarters, an appeal to examples in
nature to justify homosexuality's "naturalness" (as I have done), is
not at all convincing.[7] The irony here is that Paul himself, in
Romans 1:18-20, used nature as an example of God's deity and
creatorship. Yet modern homophobic Christians refuse to accept
this apostolic example as proof of God's diversity in his creative
pattern of sexual variation! This rejection stems from their conviction that the physical order around us has, over the milleniums,
suffered from defects initiated by humankind's fall into the subjec-
tion of sin. The resultant calamities, according to this viewpoint,
can be seen in the wildness of animals, the general hostile environment of the elements, the shortened human life spans after the
Flood, disease, and death.

Therefore, far from being a reflection of God's original plan for
sexuality, homosexual orientation is thought by some of the more
mercifully minded evangelicals to be yet another evidence of sin's
damaging inroads. In this particular line of thinking, rather than
accept their sexuality as God-given, these "afflicted" gay persons
should seek deliverance and psychiatric treatment for their
"malady." A "cure" could be accomplished through a variety of
approaches: prayer, counseling, the laying on of hands, or other
religious means. After all, they reason, if homosexuality is one of
the fruits of the curse visited upon humankind by the fall of Adam

and Eve, it stands to reason that it must be God's will to deliver such victims from the strangling clutches of this evil "degeneracy." Because this sexual deviancy is conceived by fundamentalists as being an effect of the original curse, it logically follows, in their thinking, that deliverance can be gained if we but pray and have faith. This is why it is so common to hear homophobic ministers harping on the tired theme that gay people can somehow be "set free" from their "perversion."

Interestingly enough, the "fallen sexuality" approach used by some of the fundamentalist faithful, when taken to its logical conclusion, becomes more of a hindrance to them than a help. Even if we were to accept the idea that homosexuality is one of the many examples of humanity's fragmented condition since the Fall (a position I do *not* concede), it would not justify a deliverance-needing conclusion for the gay Christian dilemma. And, oddly enough, it would declassify homosexuality from the category of "sin." Many examples can be found of inherited or acquired conditions which the Bible makes plain are consequences of the Fall, yet which no thinking Christian would be so foolhardy as to describe as manifestations of personal sin—blindness and disease, for instance. In John 9:1-5, Jesus was asked a question that reveals the prevalent concept of the time—that sickness and physical conditons such as blindness were the karmic punishment for a person's sins.[8] Jesus, however, stunned the disciples by answering that in this instance, the individual's sins did not enter into the picture. The blind man was born sightless so that God's glory could be revealed—in this case, by a miraculous cure.

From a purely biblical viewpoint, the original creation, as it came freshly formed from the hands of God, was a world free from imperfection, disorder, and death (Genesis 1:31; Romans 5:12-13). But when sin came upon the scene through our first parents' disobedience, the earth became not only a hostile environment for human beings, but was itself infected with the same deteriorating effects (Genesis 3:17-18). While it is made clear that God's ultimate purpose for his creation is that it be whole, healthful, and perfect, the corruption of the divine intent by Adam's sin did not frustrate the Lord's ultimate design for humankind's salvation and restoration.

In fact, according to Paul's interpretation, it was *God* himself who subjected the universe to deterioration, to teach us a valuable lesson on the consequences of disobedience (Romans 8:19-21). Natural calamities and human physical disorders are not necessarily products of Satan's sadistic creativity (although he is sometimes pictured as using them for his own nefarious purposes [Job 1:10-12]), but were seen as an aspect of God's reaction to sin. Therefore, it is clear that all things, including diseases and other debilitating conditions, were perceived by the scriptural authors as being tools of God, used to bring about the agonizing realization that the universal pain and mortality reaped by the human race are a result of its sin and separation from God.

> I am the Lord, and there is no other,
>> The One forming light and creating darkness,
> Causing well-being and creating calamity ["evil" KJV];
>> I am the Lord who does all these.
>>> (Isaiah 45:6b-7 NASV)

> The Lord said unto [Moses], "Who is it that gives man speech? Who makes him dumb or deaf? Who makes him clear-sighted or blind? *Is it not I, the Lord?*"
>> (Exodus 4:11 NEB [emphasis mine])

Hard as it may be to accept, the pivotal point to realize is that such a condition—whether it be blindness, disease, lameness, or, for that matter, *homosexual orientation*—while not overtly classified by Scripture as God-ordained, *can* be described as God-*given*, as Exodus 4:11 plainly emphasizes.

It is inconsistent on the part of evangelicals and fundamentalists to ostracize the homosexual as an "unnatural, perverted sinner," at the same time granting full acceptance to the blind, the cancer victim, the physically deformed, and the mentally retarded—all "unnatural" conditions when viewed from the perspective of God's perfect will. This inconsistency arises from the fact that all these human conditions have three things in common:

1. They all stem from the physical and psychological deterioration brought upon humanity through the Edenic Fall.[9]
2. These less-than-perfect conditions were not the result of a conscious choice on the part of the individual so

affected, but were, in many cases, developed in the person even prior to birth.

3. In most of these situations no cure has yet been found, except for those occasional healings which are nothing short of miraculous.

Keeping these considerations in mind, it would be necessary for homophobic Christians to categorize all such afflictions as sin and, accordingly, exclude all persons exhibiting symptoms of these maladies from full participation in the life stream of the church. This would be a logical conclusion, in light of some popular charismatic teachings concerning healing and "positive confession" theology. Many teachers of such principles will argue according to the following style of axiomatic deduction:

> By Christ's stripes we have already been
>   healed from disease (Isaiah 53:5).
> Since God is a healing God (Exodus 15:26),
>   and since Jesus healed sicknesses (Luke 4:40),
>   and since the apostle John prayed for his
>   friend to be in good health (III John 2),
>   and since the prayer of faith is said to
>   raise up the sick (James 5:14-15),
>   and since without faith it is impossible
>   to please God (Hebrews 11:6),
>   and since whatever is not of faith
>   is sin (Romans 14:23);
>   then if you doubt that it is God's will to heal
>   you of your particular affliction—
> whether blindness, cancer, or homosexuality—
> you are a practicing sinner, exercising
>   the sin of faithlessness.
> If an individual has been praying for a
>   deliverance and/or healing but has not
>   yet received it,
>   this must surely be the result of doubting
>   the veracity of the Bible's message and of
>   not believing hard enough!

This twisted theology of healing is so patently absurd in its approach to Scripture that it screams of retarded reasoning. It is surprising that at least some modern charismatic Christians who adhere to this brand of teaching have not come to realize the shortsighted shallowness of its basic tenets.

Biblical revelation underscores the truth—that because of what Christ accomplished upon the cross, complete healing, both physical and spiritual, will ultimately be ours (I Peter 2:24); but to say that it is God's will for all to be completely healed at this present moment is contrary to sound theology, even *evangelical* theology.[10] Some of the less reputable faith-healing and "deliverance" ministries so popular in certain fringe element denominations choose to carefully side-step many embarrassing passages of Scripture:

> The apostle Paul had a painful physical affliction which the Lord *refused* to heal. "I was given a physical condition which brought me pain like a stake twisting in my body. . . . Three times I pled with God about this, and asked him to take it away. 'My grace is all you need,' he said to me. 'It is in weakness that my power becomes most powerful' " (II Corinthians 12:7-9 Barclay).

> Paul recorded in his letter to the Galatians that he had a "bodily illness" when he first preached to them (Galatians 4:13 NASV).

> Paul also wrote to Timothy, explaining that during his journey, he had left one of his trusted companions sick at a certain city (II Timothy 4:20).

> Timothy frequently was seized by bouts of illness (I Timothy 5:23).

God often uses diseases and handicaps in our lives in ways we can understand only in retrospect. We know, however, that the full healing effects of Calvary will not be realized until our bodies are renewed into images of the risen Lord's own perfected body (Philippians 3:20-21). The exceptions are those rare instances when God's grace allows us actually to partake "of the powers of the Age to come" in receiving ministry from the Spirit's gift of healing within the Body of Christ (I Corinthians 12:9). So, too, those fundamentalists who are eager to classify homosexuality as a psychosexual distortion, or sickness, need to be made aware that not until the time of the Resurrection—a redemption that will cause "our bodies to be set free" (Romans 8:23 JB)—will all psychological and/or physical disorders be eliminated in the believer.

Thus if some of the more mercifully minded conservative Christians tend to view gay people as the victims of degenerative sickness, then at the very least, they should react with compassion, not with the pointed finger (Proverbs 6:13). Furthermore, if homosexual orientation is assumed by some of the evangelical rank and file to be a regretful side-effect of the human fall from innocence, it is to be considered a sickness, at most, and *not* a sin, since homosexuality is not freely chosen (despite the ignorant assertions of some fundamentalists), but is rather a spontaneous outworking of the basic identity of a person's sexual being. And if, as statistics have proved, there is no evidence of a totally transforming cure for homosexuality, then the resultant conclusion can be only that it is a variant neuro/psychosexual/biological aspect in human personal development, which must, by its very nature, fall under the scope of God's permissive will.

It seems to be the general tendency of anti-gay authors to stress the all-inclusive condemnation of homosexual acts in Romans 1. Indeed, these verses are most emphatically all-inclusive when seen from the limited vantage (or *dis*advantage) point of Paul's culturally conditioned perspective. It would certainly be advantageous at this juncture to acquire a more accurate perception of the specific and widely publicized examples of perverted depravity which must have reinforced Paul's feeling of hostility and disgust. From the context of the letter itself, it is clear, especially in his taunting put-down of Greek philosophical speculations (vv. 21-23), that Paul had Greek and Roman culture in mind. He also declared (vv. 24, 26) that the same-sex lust he was describing as being a significant part of the social fabric of that culture was, from his perspective, a manifestation of God's judicial punishment upon the God-rejecting Gentiles.

In light of this, it would seem not only cruel, but intellectually ridiculous to apply this passage to all sexual inverts. For example, a fifteen-year-old boy has grown up in the church, loves the Lord with all his heart, yet finds himself irresistibly drawn toward members of his own sex, with no corresponding desire for females at all. Shall we be so rash and insensitive as to accuse this youth of having been an idolater and tell him that he is therefore experiencing God's punishment in the form of homosexual desires? Before the zealous Christian homophobes begin to hurl passages of Scripture like bombs at their gay sisters and brothers, it would be well for them to pause and carefully consider the original context of the biblical words they often parrot in condemnation of gay "perverts."

In verses 24 and 25 of Romans 1, Paul may have been describing a specific situation well known to the Christians in Rome to whom he was writing. Significantly, in the heart of this Scripture is found what is very likely a direct reference to Roman emperor worship and the resultant depraved sexual perversions of the first-century imperial court. This is brought out best in the translation of the Concordant Literal New Testament:

> Wherefore God gives them over, in the lusts of their hearts, to the uncleanness of dishonoring their bodies among themselves, those who alter the truth of God into the lie, *and are venerated* [the Emperor, Nero Caesar?], *and offer divine service to the creature* [the cult of emperor worship?] rather than the Creator, Who is blessed for the eons! Amen! (Romans 1:24-25, CLNT [Emphasis mine]).

In light of this possibility, it is easy to see the connection between Romans 1 and II Thessalonians 2:

> And then that lawless one will be revealed ... with all the deception of wickedness for those who perish, because they did not receive the love of the truth so as to be saved. And for this reason God will send upon them a deluding influence so that they might believe what is false, in order that they all may be judged who did not believe the truth, but took pleasure in wickedness (II Thessalonians 2:8, 10-12 NASV).

The similarity in language and theme is unmistakable. In the Roman Epistle, Paul is pointing to a contemporary example of the consequences of forsaking God for the lie of idolatry, which had culminated in a blasphemous exchange, or reversal, with the human creature (in this case the emperor of Rome) claiming to be Deity and demanding that his subjects serve and worship him. In the passage from II Thessalonians, the apostle is warning the church of the ultimate manifestation of idolatry's deception, when the coming Man of Sin will "display himself to be God" (2:4) and demand the same kind of worship. A main theme in both passages is the lie of idolatry (Romans 1:25; II Thessalonians 2:11). Both narratives discuss God's judicial abandonment of sinful humans to the consequences of their idolatrous nature, their rejection of the Truth (Romans 1:24, 26, 28; II Thessalonians 2:10-12). Part and parcel of this divine abandonment was God's "giving them over" to forms of sexual depravity reflective of their irreverent role reversals in the realm of the spiritual. Paul considered these to be situations in which normally heterosexually inclined persons were finding themselves consumed with obsessive same-sex lusts. It was his understanding that God had created their godless moral state as a fitting caricature of their "upside-down" philosophies.

It is relevant to note here that even Bible scholar William Barclay, who considers homosexuality to be "the most unnatural sin," gives an accurate historical picture of the events that Paul probably had referred to when condemning the cesspool of Roman degeneracy.

> At this very time [of Paul's writings] Nero was emperor. He had taken a boy called Sporus and had had him castrated. He then married him with a full marriage ceremony and took him home in procession to his palace and lived with him as wife. With an incredible viciousness Nero had himself married a man called Pythagoras and called him his husband.[11]

That the true context of the Romans passage does not concern creation, but the worship of God as opposed to idolatrous practices, is confirmed by yet another biblical source, the Apocrypha. In the book of Wisdom are found passages that many scholars consider to be the source for Paul's polemic in Romans 1. This is especially important, for it reinforces the fact that at least some of the behavior Paul spoke about, especially the sexual misconduct, was not only considered the consequence of idolatry but, in some cases, probably was *directly related* to idolatrous cultic practices.

> Then, not content with gross error in their knowledge of God, men live in the constant warfare of ignorance and call this monstrous evil peace. *They perform ritual murders of*

children and secret ceremonies and the frenzied orgies of unnatural cults; the purity of life and marriage is abandoned.

All is in chaos ... moral corruption, *sexual perversion*, breakdown of marriage, adultery, debauchery. For the worship of idols ... is the beginning, cause, and end of every evil (Wisdom of Solomon 14:22-24, 25-28 NEB [emphasis mine]).

In comparing this passage with Paul's echoes of the same thoughts in his letter to the Romans, we find strong intimations that some of the practices were related to pagan cults. The Jerusalem Bible commentary in footnote [q], Wisdom 14, seems to support this conclusion: "Allusion to the Bacchanalian orgies of the Dionysiac Mysteries, or else to the frenzy and immorality of the Phrygian Mysteries." As has already been stated, homosexual cult prostitution was a common feature in certain mother-goddess religions of the ancient world, as Tom Horner has very thoroughly documented in his study on homosexuality in biblical times.[12] Furthermore, a comparison of Leviticus 18:21-22 with Wisdom 14:23 suggests a probable link between the prohibition of child-sacrifice and the prohibition of homosexual acts, in that the motivation for both prohibitions stems from their common relatedness with idolatry; both child-sacrifice and homosexual acts were part of various cultic pagan practices.

One must keep in mind that nearly all the homosexual activity to which Paul was exposed during his missionary journeys had to do with either idolatry, pederasty, or prostitution. It is therefore little wonder that the great apostle was so vehement in his condemnation. There is no doubt that Paul, true to the Mosaic tradition, was revolted by the licentious homosexual behavior rampant in many cities of the Roman Empire. He often regarded homosexual acts as an outward manifestation of the idolatrous nature of the Gentiles; moreover, he believed that anyone who participated in such perverted promiscuousness would never inherit the kingdom of God.

The writers of the Epistles were living in the midst of a pagan, sensual Roman world. Every kind of sexual license was known. Cities such as Corinth were "pleasure centers" where everything physical was emphasized. Such a life was hardly consistent with the Gospel of Jesus which, although it did not deny the physical, the pleasurable, the joyous, it did attempt to place "the things of this world" in perspective with "the treasures of heaven." [13]

When Paul used such terms as "dishonorable" and "degrading" when speaking of the then-current homosexual practices of Roman and Greek society, it was often for good reason, since those liaisons were for the most part *adulterous* in nature. Greek society, for instance, was primarily bisexual, in that while nearly all men were married and had fathered children, they often had other young men as lovers.[14] Even though this was perfectly acceptable from a Greek cultural perspective, it was totally unacceptable to the One True God who, according to the sacred records, had thunderously decreed, "You shall not commit adultery!" The sexual excesses of Nero's court were nothing less than perverted parodies of marriage.

Further, many pederastic practices included castration. Young boys were often purchased through the slave trade and castrated to preserve their youthful and effeminate appearance for the pleasure of their masters. Male prostitution was especially rampant in Corinth and Ephesus, and it is in his letter to the Corinthians that Paul singles out that thriving business in his list of intolerable vices.

However, due to poor and/or misleading translation, many modern Bible versions have not corrected the fallacy that in I Corinthians 6:9-11, Paul was condemning homosexuality in general. It is unfortunate that the accuracy of translation has suffered due to the powerful sway of social/sexual prejudice. Versions such as the New American Standard and the Revised Standard have poorly rendered the two separate Greek words—*malakoi* and *arsenokoitai*—with the one English designation *homosexuals*, a meaning that in all scholastic honesty must be considered inaccurate. As McNeill has pointed out, there are words in the Greek which, with far greater clarity and frequency of usage, would have left the unmistakable impression in this particular scripture that Paul's condemnation was all-encompassing in relation to homosexual acts. Yet the apostle used none of those.[15] The words he did use are ones that zero in on the specific practices of male prostitution that were so widespread in Corinth. This is brought out most exhaustively and accurately by John Boswell in his investigative masterpiece, *Christianity, Social Tolerance, and Homosex-*

uality. In the chapter titled "Lexicography and Saint Paul," Boswell authoritatively declares,

> [*arsenokoitai*], then, means male sexual agents, i.e., active male prostitutes, who were common throughout the Hellenistic world in the time of Paul. . . .
>
> Perhaps the most extensive evidence that [*arsenokoitai*] did not connote "homosexual" or even "sodomite" in the time of Paul is offered by the vast amount of writing extant on the subject of homoerotic sexuality in Greek in which this term does not occur. It is extremely difficult to believe that if the word actually meant "homosexual" . . . *no* previous or contemporary author would have used it in a way which clearly indicated this connection.[16]

After nineteen pages and fifty-four footnotes, Boswell concludes, "There is no reason to believe that either [*arsenokoitai*] or [*malakoi*] connoted homosexuality in the time of Paul or for centuries thereafter." [17] Lest anyone dismiss his statements, it should be emphasized that no more thorough work has ever been assembled in regard to Paul's words in I Corinthians 6:9 and I Timothy 1:10, for most homophobic authors utilize the standard Greek lexicons, older works which are woefully inadequate in their treatment of many words. Boswell, however, has studied the use of these words by Greek writers *contemporary* with Paul, and from this we gain a much more accurate idea of what the great apostle was trying to tell his followers.

Even the New International Version, a translation that, ironically, is being popularized by evangelicals and fundamentalists, admits that I Corinthians 6:9 relates to male prostitution: "Do you not know that the wicked will not inherit the kingdom of God? Do not be deceived: Neither the sexually immoral nor idolaters nor adulterers *nor male prostitutes nor homosexual offenders* . . . will inherit the kingdom of God" (emphasis mine). Gay Christians, in this instance, would be the first to agree with the apostle. Male prostitution is just as degrading and just as great a denial of the divine intention of sexual fulfillment through love as is female prostitution. In light of Boswell's research, it is interesting to note that NIV translators correctly derived the meaning of male prostitution in this verse, but from the incorrect word! They apparently mistakenly assumed that *malakoi* had reference to prostitution, while *arsenokoitai* was describing what they vaguely translated as "homosexual offenders" (the prostitutes' clientele? child molesters? rapists?—"offenders" against whom?) Actually, as we have observed, it is *arsenokoitai* that means *male prostitution*. *Malakoi*, the word that precedes it, means literally "*soft, voluptuous,* [and] appears in this connexion to signify general addiction to sins of the flesh." [18] This coincides with Boswell's conclusion that "the soundest inference is that [*malakoi*] refers to general moral weakness, with no specific connection to homosexuality." [19] Furthermore, the assertion often made by anti-gay exegetes to the effect that these two words are technical descriptions of the active and passive sex roles in homosexual relations and that their use therefore condemns all homosexual acts is, according to Boswell, "fanciful and unsubstantiated by lexicographical evidence." [20]

This is not, of course, meant to imply that Paul would have looked kindly on any kind of homosexual expression. But it does demonstrate that many of the apostle's condemnations were not as general and sweeping in scope as some modern translations have led us to believe. On the contary, they were written to combat specific sexual activities which, to the mind of Paul, were reprehensible, not only because of their homosexual nature, but because of their general relatedness to vice and prostitution.

When Paul stated in I Corinthians 6:11 that some of the Corinthian Christians had been delivered from the various practices he had mentioned ("and such *were* some of you"), it is evident that he had in mind, among other things, professions of sexual vice—not inborn or psychological orientation of human sexuality. When homophobic "deliverance" ministries use this passage as a standing promise from God that persons can be "set free" from their homosexually inverted condition, it is nothing less than a cruel misuse of Scripture.

In I Timothy 1:10 is found Paul's only other reference to alleged homosexual practices. However, this text simply consists of another list of vices and assorted immoralities, in which Paul once again makes use of that now notorious word *arsenokoitai*, with apparently the same meaning he had attached to it when addressing the Corinthian church. It would be well to mention that there have been fascinating suggestions that the apostle's listing of "kidnappers" immediately after male prostitutes could have been intentional. The reference could have been to those who made a lucrative living by stealing young boys and selling them to wealthy pedophiles who avidly sought sexual enjoyment and companionship from these adolescents. As the boys grew older, many often resorted to prostitution as a means of livelihood. This notion is totally unprovable, but it does remain an intriguing possibility.

In the final analysis, what, then, can be said of the New Testament's understanding of homosexuality? As far as homosexual inversion is concerned, the Christian Scriptures say absolutely nothing. It is certain, if not obvious from the writings themselves, that homosexual orientation as we understand it today, in light of the complex psychological, biological, and sociological givens, was unknown by Christians of the early church. Nor should we of the twentieth century be so unrealistically demanding as to expect first-century Christian leaders to have been aware of an inherent condition 1,900 years removed from the realm of scientific and psychological discovery. It is unfortunate that modern fundamentalist thought has done just that—it has attributed a form of divine omniscience to all biblical writers concerning any subject or social phenomenon that they happened to touch upon in the course of their dissertations.

What the New Testament *does* address, however, is the morality of homosexual acts as they were viewed by the apostles in the immediate context of their own religious upbringing and cultural expectations. Without a doubt, male prostitution, homosexual lust, and hedonistic heterosexual degeneracy, manifested through participation in same-sex activity, are all unequivocally condemned in the Epistles, and rightfully so. "We may very well say that what the Apostle was driving at was the evil of promiscuous sexuality, prostitution, and a general refusal to accept love as the clue to all genuinely human sexual expression." [21]

But what of gay *love*? This is the ultimate issue. There are numerous authors sympathetic to the gay Christian cause who have attempted to answer this question; some of them, as I noted before, have done so rather inadequately. The whole purpose of my examination of Paul's writings has been to emphasize the essential point, which is often not given proper attention in determining Paul's attitude toward homosexual love that expresses itself in the context of sexual acts. That point resides primarily in one word—*assumption*; since the apostle *assumed* heterosexuality to be the only natural or God-ordained orientation, he could view homosexual acts only as forms of degenerate activity. As has been shown, Paul's assumption that all persons were heterosexual by nature and his resultant conclusions in Romans 1 cannot be applied to the psychobiological phenomenon of constitutional homosexual inversion, since Paul had no knowledge of its existence. The most we can legitimately interpret from the apostle's words, then, is that lustful homosexual acts, engaged in by persons whose original or normal sexual inclinations are heterosexual, are observable examples of the spiritual and idolatrous chaos of a God-rejecting society. In this, I would concur.

It seems apparent from Paul's writings that the idea of homosexual acts as expressions of genuine love between two persons never entered into the formulation of his conclusions. Such conduct seemed always to be associated with lust and degeneracy, not love. It is not surprising that Paul never distinguished between gay love and lust, simply because of the logic of his presuppositions: If homosexual activity had its origin in pagan idolatry and rebelliousness, then any expression of sexual love through the medium of such practices could surely be no less perverted than other, less affectionate forms of homosexual licentiousness.

Again, we must underline the fact that Paul's assumptions, based as they were upon the limited understandings of his time and the prejudicial influence of his Jewish upbringing, created limitations within the apostle's thinking that we must recognize if we are to accurately interpret his teaching in a theologically relevant way. In the words of James B. Nelson,

> What then should we make of Paul's moral judgment in this case? Perhaps we should just accept him for what he was: a faithful apostle and a profound interpreter of the central message of the gospel, yet one who was also a fallible and historically conditioned human being. . . . If the norm of the new humanity in Jesus Christ together with our best current moral wisdom and empirical knowledge would cause us to question some of Paul's moral convictions about the status of women and about the institution of human slavery, surely his moral judgments about homosexual acts ought not be exempt.

The central biblical message regarding sexuality seems

clear enough. Like every other good gift, it can be misused. The idolatrous dishonoring of God inevitably results in the dishonoring of persons, and faithfulness to God will result in sexual expression which honors the personhood of the other.[22]

It is also paramount that we keep in our perspective that such well-intentioned, yet as we now know mistaken conclusions on Paul's part, do not apply to genuine homosexual inverts today. Since such psychosexual orientation was unknown to the biblical writers for what it is—a genuine and natural variant human sexual condition—it is clear that, *as such*, this issue was never addressed by New Testament authors.

NOTES

1. J. Rinzema, *The Sexual Revolution* (Grand Rapids: William B. Eerdmans Publishing Co., 1974), p. 105. Used by permission.
2. David Field, *The Homosexual Way—A Christian Option?* (Downers Grove, Ill.: InterVarsity Press, Revised ed. © 1979 by David Field. Used by permission of InterVarsity Press, Downers Grove, IL 60515. 1979), pp. 29-30.
3. Wainwright Churchill, *Homosexual Behavior Among Males* (Englewood Cliffs, N.J.: Prentice-Hall, 1967), pp. 67-69, partially quoted from D.J. West, *Homosexuality*. London: Gerald Duckworth, 1955.
4. John J. McNeill, S.J., *The Church and the Homosexual* (Kansas City: Sheed, Andrews & McMeel, 1976), pp., 53-56. Used by permission. This permission applies also to all succeeding quotations.
5. John Boswell, *Christianity, Social Tolerance and Homosexuality* (Chicago/London: © 1980 by The University of Chicago Press), pp. 111-12.
6. Jerry R. Kirk, *The Homosexual Crisis in the Mainline Church* (Thomas Nelson: Nashville/ New York; 1978), p. 59.
7. "An appeal to nature means nothing in a fallen world" (Richard F. Lovelace, *Homosexuality and the Church* [Old Tappan, N.J.: Fleming H. Revell Co., 1978], p. 93).
8. The assumption of reincarnation is inherent in the disciples' question, "Rabbi, who sinned, *this man* or his parents, *for him to have been born* blind?" For the man's sins to have had any determining factor in the circumstances of his birth, they would of necessity had to have been committed in a *previous* life. It must be remembered that certain limited concepts of reincarnation were not foreign to the speculations and beliefs of many in first-century Judaism (Matthew 11:14; 17:9-13; 16:13-15).
9. This is assuming for the sake of argument that homosexuality is, in fact, a result of the Fall, a position I have made clear that I do not concede.
10. Peg Rankin, *Yet Will I Trust Him* (Glendale, Calif.: Regal Books, G/L Publications, 1980), pp. 68-74. © Copyright 1980, Regal Books, Ventura, CA 93006. Used by permission. This permission also applies to all succeeding quotations.
11. William Barclay, trans. and interpreter, *The Letters to the Corinthians*, rev. ed. (Philadelphia: The Westminster Press, 1975), pp. 53-54. Copyright © 1975, William Barclay. Used by permission.

12. Tom Horner, *Jonathan Loved David*, (Philadelphia: The Westminster Press, 1978), pp. 59-70.
13. Clinton R. Jones, *What About Homosexuality?* (Nashville/New York: Thomas Nelson, 1972), pp. 38-39.
14. Letha Scanzoni and Virginia Ramey Mollenkott, *Is the Homosexual My Neighbor?* (San Francisco: Harper & Row, 1978), p. 66.
15. McNeill, *The Church and the Homosexual*, p. 53.
16. Boswell, *Christianity, Social Tolerance, Homosexuality*, pp. 344, 345.
17. Ibid., p. 353.
18. W. Robertson Nicholl, ed., *The Expositor's Greek Testament* (Grand Rapids: Wm. B. Eerdman's Publishing Co., 1979), vol. 2, p. 52. Used by permission.
19. Boswell, *Christianity, Social Tolerance, Homosexuality*, p. 340.
20. Ibid., p. 341.
21. Norman Pittenger, *Time for Consent: A Christian's Approach to Homosexuality*, 3rd rev. ed. (London: SMC Press, 1970, 1976), p. 105.
22. James B. Nelson, *Embodiment: An Approach to Sexuality and Christian Theology* (Minneapolis: Augsburg Publishing House, 1978), p. 188. Copyright Augsburg Publishing House. Reprinted by permission. This permission also applies to all succeeding quotations.

Chapter **8**

Ordinances and Outcasts

Of all the issues confronting the church today, most observers agree that homosexuality is and will remain for quite some time the most perplexing, persistent topic troubling the people of God. Strangely enough, the scriptural answer will not be found in the popularly used, but for the most part misunderstood passages from Romans 1 and I Corinthians 6. Devout Christians, both gay and non-gay, have written convincingly (and sometimes vehemently) on opposite sides of the issue as related to biblical interpretation, and the theological dust shows no sign of settling, as the very presence of this book indicates. This is all the more reason we should seek to discover another key by which to explore the validity of the gay Christian viewpoint.

Tucked away in the pages of the book of Acts is an interesting incident which helped to change the course of the early church. It began with alienation, but ended with acceptance. Yet it was only a miracle of God that effected the transformation. In Acts 10 and 11, there is a story about a vision experienced by the apostle Peter one day as he was praying. The experience was very disturbing, but the Spirit eventually impressed upon him its full implication, prompting him to radically change his viewpoints about other people, as well as his life-style. This, of course, greatly upset the religious fundamentalists of the early church, who demanded an explanation from Peter for his seemingly scandalous behavior: He had openly associated with "unclean" Gentiles.

When Peter came up to Jerusalem the Jews [Hebrew Chris-
tians] criticized him and said, "So you have been visiting
the uncircumcised and eating with them, have you?" Peter
in reply gave them the details point by point: "One day,
when I was in the town of Jaffa," he began, "I fell into a
trance as I was praying and had a vision of something like a
big sheet being let down from heaven by its four corners.
This sheet reached the ground quite close to me. I watched
it intently and saw all sorts of animals and wild beasts—
everything possible that could walk, crawl or fly. Then I
heard a voice that said to me, 'Now, Peter; kill and eat!' But I
answered: Certainly not, Lord; nothing profane or unclean
has ever crossed my lips. And a second time the voice
spoke from heaven, 'What God has made clean, you have no
right to call profane.' This was repeated three times, before
the whole of it was drawn up to heaven again.

"Just at that moment, three men stopped outside the
house where we were staying; they had been sent from
Caesarea to fetch me, and the Spirit told me to have no
hesitation about going back with them. The six brothers
here came with me as well, and we entered the man's
house. He told us he had seen an angel standing in his
house who said, 'Send to Jaffa and fetch Simon known as
Peter; he has a message for you that will save you and your
entire household.'

"I had scarcely begun to speak when the Holy Spirit
came down on them in the same way as it came on us at
the beginning, and I remembered that the Lord had said,
'John baptized with water, but you will be baptized with
the Holy Spirit.' I realized then that God was giving them
the identical thing he gave to us when we believed in the
Lord Jesus Christ; and who was I to stand in God's way?"

This account satisfied them, and they gave glory to God.
"God" they said "can evidently grant even the pagans the
repentance that leads to life" (Acts 11:2b-18 JB).

The parallels between this story and the situation that confronts
the church today are indeed striking. We can well compare Peter's
dumbfounded reply of horrified amazement, "Certainly not, Lord!"
with the current reaction of numerous Christians to the mere

mention of the possibility that homosexuals might be openly tolerated and admitted to the full fellowship of the church. In the
context of the Acts narrative, the vision of unclean foods, and
God's subsequent declaration that they had now been cleansed,
did not pertain solely to the dietary laws of the Old Testament. The
forbidden foods fittingly represented all the divergent races of
humankind that devout Jews had hitherto relegated to the same
ritually contaminated category as pigs and snakes—unclean. This
Peter clearly perceived, "and [he] said to them, 'You know it is
forbidden for Jews to mix with people of another race and visit
them, *but God has made it clear to me that I must not call anyone
profane or unclean*'" (Acts 10:28 JB [emphasis mine]).

Under the Old Covenant dispensation, all non-Jews were ex-
cluded from the "chosenness" of God's acceptance unless they
entered into Israel's covenant through circumcision and conformance to the Mosaic Law. The principle Peter gleaned from his
vision of creeping beasts encompassed the very essence of all discrimination against those made in the image of God: "The aboli-
tion of Jewish ceremonial barriers was pressed home in the vision
with special reference to food laws, *but Peter soon grasped that its
range was much wider.*"[1] (emphasis mine)

The Jewish community in the very early apostolic Church had
to learn a lesson so important that God used both a vision and a
voice—the audible voice of the Lord—to impress them. This was
no small matter, for God was conveying to Peter, and through him
to the whole church, a principle which, when its implications are
understood, will terrify most fundamentalists to the tips of their
toes.

Those who are familiar with the axioms of evangelical/fun-
damentalist rhetoric will surely recognize the following para-
phrased law of literalistic interpretation:

> If a doctrine, teaching, or religious vision of a person is in
> any way contradictory of that which God has revealed in
> the holy Scriptures as being his will, then such dogmas
> and/or visions cannot be from the Lord. They are either
> satanically inspired or the result of human misunderstand-
> ing and delusion.

If the apostle Peter had adhered to such a series of theological
presuppositions, he no doubt would have rejected the vision of

unclean creatures as being an insidious attempt on the part of the devil to deceive him into disobeying God's Law. Such a conclusion would have been only logical, had Peter been a biblical literalist, since the Mosaic injunctions forbade the eating of unclean beasts (Leviticus 11). After all, Peter would have reasoned, why would God command me to do that which is a sin under the Law and against the clear admonitions of the holy Scriptures? Furthermore, the predominant meaning of the vision, according to Peter, was that association with Gentiles, which heretofore had been unlawful because of scriptural injunctions (Joshua 23:6-7), was now the will of God for the Jewish Christians. *In other words, Peter's vision served as a divine abrogation of scriptural authority with reference to the instructions regarding Jewish/Gentile fellowship.* The book of Acts tells us that the Lord superceded the scriptural regulations by means of a visionary communication of his will.

We can now perceive why a fundamentalist would be so disturbed by this story. Peter did not depend on the Scriptures as his ultimate authority in determining whether the vision came from God, for the vision itself *contradicted* the Hebrew Scriptures. What then was Peter's supreme criterion for determining the authenticity of the vision? There can be only one answer. It was the apostle's *inner witness and knowledge* that the voice he heard was that of the Lord, and he had learned through his years with Jesus to follow that call, whether or not he fully understood the implications. It was Jesus himself who had declared, "My sheep hear My voice, and I know them, and they follow Me" (John 10:27 NASV).

The problem with most evangelicals and fundamentalists today is that they have substituted a blind reliance upon the Bible for a faith that relies on spiritual perception, through which the individual Christian may be always alert to hear what the Spirit is saying in the *now* of human history. In fact, many Christians prefer the crutch of biblical literalism, because by relying on the "Good Book" for all the answers, they are no longer forced to exercise their spiritual discernment in determining the sources and/or moral nature of the many conflicting winds of doctrine that blow through the citadels of Christianity. The bottom line is clear: God does not always move by established biblical standards. God has not been boxed in by the Bible, as much as conservative Christians may wish that were true.

Had Peter followed present evangelical guidelines—those of

Sola Scriptura—for determining the truthfulness of visions and revelations, his reaction to the vision on the rooftop would have been far different, resulting in the hopeless confinement of the Christian Church within the restricting mold of a minor apocalyptic sect of Judaism. Had Peter put his total trust in the Scriptures of his past upbringing and allowed them to be the sole factor in his evaluation of spiritual validity, it is doubtful that he would have made the decisions or written the new Scriptures that were instrumental in leading the church into the future. In like manner, if contemporary Christian leaders would allow the still, small voice which we call the inner witness of the Spirit (Romans 8:16) to take precedence over their entrenched societal prejudices, they would begin to find themselves far more open to the reality of God's gracious reaffirmation in the lives of so many in the gay community.

Gay people have much in common with the Gentiles of Peter's day who, like Cornelius, desired to walk with God but were often faced with opposition and outright rejection by the Jews, who insisted that they submit to the multitude of requirements set forth in the rigors of Mosaic Law. But the New Testament writers tell us that that attitude of heart and the resultant exclusion came to an abrupt end in God's sovereign economy of dealing with humanity. The scriptural injunctions that had been given to the Hebrews were no longer to be followed. In essence, the authority of the written biblical pronouncements bowed before the higher authority of the living Word of the Lord, manifested through visions, revelations, and the anointed teachings given to the people of the New Covenant through its God-predestined leaders (Joel 2:28-29; Acts 2:42; I Thessalonians 2:13).

Ironically, even though evangelical charismatics and other neo-Pentecostals emphasize the validity of visions and new revelations for our day, they nevertheless imprison the spiritually spontaneous and guiding effect that such a belief could generate in the church by insisting that any revelations which contradict or seem puzzlingly different from some of the already existing body of Holy Writ must be judged as false teaching. Had the early Christians held to such a view, they would have resoundingly rejected the liberating message of Peter's vision.

The book of Acts further records that the early believers felt that Peter's vision and message was indisputably confirmed, not by an appeal to Scripture, but by the physically observable evidence that the Gentiles had been baptized with the Holy Spirit, complete with the gifts of prophecy and tongues (Acts 10:44-48). Peter's reaction to such a demonstration of God's movement in their midst was to inquire how anyone could now doubt that Gentiles should be accepted into the Covenant Community, since they had received the gift of the Holy Spirit in the same manner as they themselves had.

Sadly, modern charismatics and fundamentalist Pentecostals have been seemingly unable to correlate that first-century incident with the present-day reality of numerous Christian gays who are receiving the marvelous infilling of the Spirit, including the gift of speaking in tongues. This is not wishful fantasy—it is fact. This presents modern charismatics with a dilemma, due to their stubborn reluctance to follow Peter's example of taking the Holy Spirit's baptism of an individual as a definite indication that God has freely and approvingly accepted that person as an obedient believer and a recognized member of the New Covenant Community.

The apostles declared that God gives the Holy Spirit only to those who obey him (Acts 5:32). Therefore, since many practicing homosexual Christians are today receiving the baptism of the Holy Spirit, something the Bible says is given *only* to those who seek to obey the Lord, charismatics have only two alternatives: to accept gay believers into the full fellowship of the church, just as Peter accepted the Gentiles, or to deny the reality of those Spirit baptisms as being demonic manifestations for the purpose of deception. This last option (which many have chosen to embrace) puts the fundamentalists fearfully on very dangerous ground, for according to their own teaching on the subject, people who attribute to Satan the works of the Holy Spirit run the risk of committing the unpardonable sin. The evangelical charismatic community needs to thoughtfully reassess this issue and make some tough decisions. Otherwise, they risk divine condemnation for slandering the regenerative works of God in the lives of countless gay believers.

Christians are called first and foremost to be the visible expression of God's love, forgiveness, and faithfulness in the world by being the active extension of the New Covenant-in-Community. Unfortunately, most Christians have little understanding of the radical difference between the Old Covenant under the Mosaic

Law and the New Covenant under the dispensation of grace. The former was legalistic, restrictive, condemning, and inherently faulty as a means to insure salvation, because of human inability to accomplish the covenant requirements (Romans 8:3). But we are told that Jesus established a New Covenant through his blood shed on the cross, a powerful evidence of God's sacrificial self-giving in order to demonstrate to us his loving intentions for our eventual redemption and wholeness as completed images of the Divine.

One of the frequently overlooked qualities of our New Covenant in Christ is its *inclusiveness*. In the Old Testament we find that the covenant of Sinai was primarily exclusive, in that its aim was to perfect a specific "chosen" people as an example of God's holiness operative in human history (Exodus 19:5-6). Yet it was the prophet Isaiah who spoke of a future covenant that God would make with his people—a covenant that would encompass those very people whom the Mosaic Law prohibited from entering into the worship activities of Israel!

In the New Testament Epistles, Paul once even made reference to the fact that in the Temple at Jerusalem, Gentiles were not allowed to pass beyond a certain wall for the purpose of worship (Ephesians 2:14). But in the same passage, he went on to state that through the blood of Jesus, the unifying Lamb of God, there was now opportunity for worship by Gentile as well as Jew, without the need for continuing conformance to the Mosaic Law. This was something unheard of under the former covenant. However, in the prophecy of Isaiah, we find another class of people who are eulogized, comforted, and even promised great stature in the kingdom of God.

> Thus says the Lord,
> "Preserve justice, and do righteousness,
> For My salvation is about to come
> And My righteousness to be revealed.
> "How blessed is the man who does this,
> And the son of man who takes hold of it;
> Who keeps from profaning the sabbath,
> And keeps his hand from doing any evil."
> Let not the [Gentile] who has
>   joined himself to the LORD say,

"The LORD will surely separate me from
    His people."
Neither let the *eunuch* say, "Behold, I
    am a dry tree."
For thus says the LORD,
"To the *eunuchs* who keep My sabbaths,
And choose what pleases Me,
And hold fast My covenant,
To them I will give in My house and
    within My walls a memorial,
And a name better than that of sons
    and daughters;
I will give them an everlasting name
    which will not be cut off.

"Also the [Gentiles] who join themselves
    to the LORD,
To minister to Him, and to love the name
    of the Lord,
To be His servants, every one who keeps
    from profaning the sabbath,
And holds fast My covenant;
Even those I will bring to My holy
    mountain,
And make them joyful in My house of
    prayer. . . ."
The LORD GOD, who gathers the dispersed
    of Israel, declares,
"Yet others I will gather to them, to those
    already gathered" (Isaiah 56:1-8 NASV [emphasis mine]).

This passage deserves careful examination for several reasons. We
should pay special attention to the time set for the fulfillment of
this prophecy. According to the first verse, it would be during the
era in which God's salvation and righteousness were fully revealed. To the writers of the Christian Scriptures, that supreme
revelation was the coming of Jesus as the Messiah.[2] So we see that
the time element was projected as being that of the Christian
dispensation of grace.

    This is further reflected in the comforting and conciliatory attitude of God toward the rejected and outcast of the earth. These verses state that not only will the Gentiles ("foreigners") be honored and accepted in the kingdom of God, but so also will the people known as "eunuchs." Those ancient Jews who first heard or read these proclamations of Isaiah were no doubt scandalized, and for good reason: The Law of Moses forbade the participation of eunuchs in the religious rites of the Hebrews. "No one who is wounded by crushing of the testicles, or has his male organ cut off, shall enter the assembly of the Lord" (Deuteronomy 23:1). Such emasculation automatically rendered a man ineligible to participate in the religious life of the society. The Law of Moses, stated above, is most explicit on this point. For this reason, the promises of acceptance and even exaltation for eunuchs in the kingdom of the Messiah, attributed to the Lord by Isaiah, became all the more audacious and religiously suspect to the average Jew of orthodox persuasion.

So once again, we find a situation where Scripture reversed itself. Evidently God does not have nearly so extreme a view on the "unalterableness" of biblical instructions and practices as do the fundamentalists, as can be seen by comparing Deuteronomy 23:1 and Isaiah 56:1-8.

Even more important in their bearing upon the issue of homosexual tolerance in the church are the varied definitions given by Jesus himself of the types of people who qualify as eunuchs:

> There are eunuchs who were born that way from their mother's womb; and there are eunuchs who were made eunuchs by men; and there are also eunuchs who made themselves eunuchs for the sake of the kingdom of heaven. He who is able to accept this, let him accept it (Matthew 19:12 NASV).

William Barclay's translation gives us even more illumination in respect to the meaning of this rather curious and obscure verse that is unlike any other in the Gospels:

> There are some who have been born incapable of marriage. There are some who by the action of men have been made incapable of marriage. There are some who have voluntarily made marriage impossible for themselves for the sake of the

Kingdom of Heaven. Let the man who is able to accept this principle accept it.

The NASV expression "eunuchs who were born that way from their mother's womb" was translated by Barclay as "some who have been born incapable of marriage." There is, perhaps, no description in the Bible that could more accurately be applied to what we today would call constitutional homosexual inversion. Of the three categories listed by Jesus, two are very easily understood. Those who had been made eunuchs by men through castration were greatly in evidence in the ancient world and often were given high positions of trust in regulating the harems of royalty. Those who voluntarily abstained from marriage for the sake of the Kingdom clearly were persons like the apostle Paul, who considered marriage to be a hinderance to the fullest expression of their ministry (I Corinthians 7). But those whom our Lord designates as "eunuchs from their mother's womb" cannot so easily be identified by interpreters. For persons to be incapable or unsuited for marriage from birth suggests a number of possibilities, ranging from those born with genital deformities to the sexually indifferent, or perhaps even the mentally retarded, but none of these explanations is satisfying or definitive. It seems highly unlikely that Jesus would top his list of eunuch categories with an extremely rare phenomenon, whereas his other categories were both well known and readily identifiable by his contemporaries in Roman and Middle Eastern culture.

The very possible and most stimulating explanation of Jesus' words lies in the likelihood that he was very insightfully describing, among others, those who were incapable of heterosexual marriage due to their homosexual orientation, a condition he said was theirs from birth. This is not as farfetched as it might seem, especially when one takes into account the fact that many eunuchs in the ancient world were said to be homosexually inclined. Therefore, for our Lord to use this word in reference to persons of homosexual persuasion is not at all improbable. It should also be remembered that due to Christ's spiritual insight and the depth of his psychological understanding of "what makes people tick," described time and again in the pages of the Gospels, there is every reason to believe that his discernment in this area of human sexuality went far beyond the limitations of the restrictive levitical legislation of the Holiness Code.

Whether Jesus specifically had in mind people of homosexual orientation is, in the last analysis, not provable with any great degree of certainty. It is, however, a very distinct possibility. And it should be remembered that the category of those incapable of marriage, while not limited to homosexuals, nevertheless certainly *does* include many of them. Most gay people have very little attraction to the opposite sex, and while there are some who may be able to physically consummate a heterosexual relationship (as some have felt forced to do because of societal expectations and pressure), overwhelming evidence indicates that they are, for the most part, incapable of sustaining a healthy and satisfying marriage with a member of the opposite sex. In any event, it is plainly evident that homosexuals make up a considerable percentage of that "eunuch" class of people, who, for various reasons, are incapable of heterosexual marriage.

In light of these findings and speculations, the prophecy we have been considering can be said to have a most appropriate application to gay Christian believers. This significance was not lost on the keenly perceptive John J. McNeill, when he examined that excerpt from Isaiah's pen.

> The application of this prophecy to the homosexual can be defended, because the term "eunuch" in the New Testament is used not only in its literal sense ... but also in a symbolic sense for all those who for various reasons do not marry and bear children. ...
>
> It should come as no surprise, then, that the first group of outcasts of Israel that the Holy Spirit includes within the new covenant community is symbolized by the Ethiopian eunuch [Acts 8:26-39]. It is the Spirit who takes the initiative by leading Philip to the encounter with the Ethiopian eunuch of the court of Candace. The eunuch believes in Christ as the Messiah and receives baptism and the Spirit and rides on into history "full of joy." The symbolism of the passage is quite obvious. The Holy Spirit takes the initiative in leading the new Christian community to include among its members those who were excluded for sexual reasons from the Old Testament community.[3]

The promised covenant which the Lord would make with the newly accepted "eunuchs of the Kingdom" is not without its conditions, however. Isaiah (56:4) wrote that the only eunuchs whom God would exalt and welcome into his divine presence were those who

1. keep My sabbaths
2. choose what pleases Me
3. hold fast My covenant.

We must turn to the pages of the New Testament to gain proper insight into the meaning of these requirements, in light of Christian prophetic fulfillment.

The early Christians regarded the various sabbaths enjoined under the Old Testament as prophetic observances, which had been symbolically fulfilled in the person of Christ himself. "You must not therefore let anyone criticize you ... with regard to the alleged correct observance of festivals, new moons and sabbaths. These things are no more than the shadow of the things to come; the reality belongs to Christ" (Colossians 2:16-17 Barclay).

Jesus personally confirmed this in his earthly ministry when he scandalized the Jews by proclaiming himself to be the Lord of the sabbath (Mark 2:27); as Lord of the sabbath, he was the personal embodiment of all that the sabbath symbolized. Keep in mind that the sabbath was commanded primarily as a day of total rest, with all work and physical labor explicitly prohibited (Exodus 20:8-11). But Jesus made it clear that the command to rest on the seventh day had but pointed to his own ministry and his office as Lord of the sabbath; his purpose was to minister spiritual rest to the weary and heavy-laden—those who had labored too long under the harsh taskmaster of sin and its resultant calamities. "Come to Me, all who are weary and heavy-laden, and I will give you rest. Take My yoke upon you, and learn from Me, for I am gentle and humble in heart; and YOU SHALL FIND REST FOR YOUR SOULS (Matthew 11:28-29 NASV [emphasis mine]).

When we accept Jesus Christ—accept him as our Lord and Savior—we begin at that moment to enter into the "Sabbath-rest" of God, for we have put our burdens at the feet of Christ and have begun a walk of faith, confident that God's grace alone is sufficient for our personal salvation. Yet, ironically, we are encouraged by the writer of the book of Hebrews to laboriously strive in order to enter that rest of the Spirit which redemption makes possible: "There remains therefore a Sabbath rest for the people of God. For the one who has entered His rest has himself also rested from his works, as God did from His. Let us therefore be diligent to enter that rest" (Hebrews 4:9-11a NASV).

This is a message that is especially applicable to the many gay Christians being continuously harassed by homophobic fundamentalists who virtually insist that one can be saved or retain salvation only by observing the works of the Law (i.e., Leviticus 18:22) and by practicing the legalistic commandments of psychosexual denial. When gays are told that in order to "get to heaven," their acceptance of Christ must be predicated upon renouncing and denying the physical expression of their sexuality, it is no wonder many of them find it hard to believe that they can simply lean on Jesus' promise to the heavy-laden that "whosoever will" may come, apart from any condition of attempted self-reform. What we really need is rest from the tiresome and futile labor of trying to change what and who we are by God's design. It is the job of the Holy Spirit to mold us into the image of Jesus Christ; yet the Spirit is not sent to us for the purpose of negating our personhood, of which our sexuality is a part, but to transform it, as an aspect of wholesome humanity, into a radiant expression of our individual and unique creatureliness. For this reason, it is imperative that Christian gays, or, if you will, the Lord's "eunuchs," remember to figuratively keep God's sabbaths by learning to rest in the assurance that "we are accepted in the Beloved" (Ephesians 1:6) solely by God's grace and gracious predestination, which has circumvented our need to give up that which he has given us as a gift—our sexual identity as gay people.

The godly eunuchs were also commanded, in the passage from Isaiah, to do what pleases the Lord and to hold fast his covenant. This speaks to us of Christian discipleship in our walk with God. While it is certainly true that our salvation is based entirely upon the operative grace of God, it nevertheless is equally true that the Lord Jesus Christ desires his followers to be characterized by the fruits of the Spirit and the good works of righteousness.

> For we are His workmanship, created in Christ Jesus for good works, which God prepared beforehand, that we should walk in them . . . so that those who have believed God may be careful to engage in good deeds. . . . The fruit of the Spirit is love, joy, peace, patience, kindness, goodness,

faithfulness, gentleness, self-control; against such things there is no law (Ephesians 2:10; Titus 3:8b; Galatians 5:22-23 NASV).

An army of devoted gay believers, trying their best to follow in the footsteps of Christ (I Peter 2:21), could do more than any amount of mere verbal witnessing to influence those in the secular gay community to open their hearts to the love of Jesus Christ. Again, it was the writer to the Hebrews who recognized that we must match our words with a consistent life-style: "Let us hold fast the confession of our hope without wavering, for He who promised is faithful; and let us consider how to stimulate one another to love and good deeds" (Hebrews 10:23-24 NASV).

We have been sent by Christ to be the visible symbols of his life at work in the world, but if the Christ within us is all but invisible to those around us due to our lack of Christian testimony in both word and deed, we will emerge eventually as vessels of dishonor in the household of God. As an example, if our moral approach to personal values is no different from that of those we seek to convert, the unbeliever will see no valid reason to lead a life based upon the higher moral and spiritual principles of the Christian faith. In essence, we must practice what we preach.

We see, then, that the great prophecy in Isaiah concerning the eunuchs of God makes it abundantly evident that God's attitude toward those of us who have been derogatorily labeled fruits, faggots, dykes, queers, and pansies, those of us who have long been considered the sexual outcasts of society, is one of loving acceptance through the open arms of Jesus Christ, our true Friend. Christ has come to give us a sense of personal dignity based upon the value that God has placed upon us. We can accept ourselves because we have been accepted by the Lord.

God is continuing to unfold the divine purposes of his will for us, leading us into newer depths of insight. The Lord has always worked through the medium of progressive revelation. It was the prophets who expanded the truths contained in the Law of Moses. It was Christ who magnified the inner meaning of the prophets. It was the apostle Paul and the other disciples who more fully interpreted the life, death, and resurrection of the Lord Jesus. And God has not yet finished. The Lord is bringing us into a new understanding of our sexuality and of the inclusiveness of Christ's love for us as gay people, through the increasing witness of God's Spirit stirring within our own spirits.

When all is said and done, we are left with the overwhelming conviction that the accusations leveled by the Moral Majority and their variety of fundamentalist supporters against homosexuality, and against gay people in general, are nothing more than paper tigers.

We have heard, all too often, the rantings of culturally conditioned Christians who do not hesitate to hide behind the smokescreen of "scriptural loyalty" to justify their homophobic prejudices. Whether it be the hyped rhetoric of money-hungry television evangelists, eager to capitalize on the fears of the uneducated, or the venomous literature of the New Right religious press, the message of doom and damnation remains the same: Unless militant gays repent before God and turn from their sexual "wickedness," they will all die in sin and go to the Devil's hell. It is the verdict of these fundamentalists that the only hope for homosexuals who claim that their life-style is compatible with the teachings of Jesus is to renounce such a "Devil-inspired heresy." Most homophobic preachers believe that nothing short of copious tears of remorse, shed in a sea of sorrow at the foot of the cross, will prevent the omnipotent hand of divine indignation from pronouncing the dreadful declaration of eternal damnation, consigning gays forever to their fate as "crispy critters" in the pit of God's everlasting barbecue.

Such self-righteous tirades may sound threatening, loaded as they are with generous portions of hell-fire and brimstone, but upon closer examination, they contain no substantial validity within the realm of responsible theology. So what should be our conclusion?

> We no longer have ... sufficient theological grounds for perpetuating a destructive attitude. This does not mean that some homosexual relations are not unhealthy, unchristian, and sinful. It simply means that homosexuality can exist in healthy, Christian, and graced forms. ...
>
> There are different ways of being homosexual and different ways of being heterosexual. Christian understanding praises relationships seen in the context of love, fidelity, permanence, and living in Christ through the Spirit.[4]

And in the words of our Savior and one of his greatest apostles, "You will know the truth, and the truth will make you free." ". . . For freedom Christ has set us free; stand fast therefore, and do not submit again to a yoke of slavery" (John 8:32; Galatians 5:1-2 RSV). The yoke of bondage that has been imposed on so many of our gay sisters and brothers by the churchly establishment cannot continue to be tolerated. The freedom of knowing Jesus Christ as Lord and Savior has liberated us from the lonely despair that so often characterized our lives when we were the rejects of prejudiced churches.

"Those whom the world thinks common and contemptible are the ones that God has chosen—those who are nothing at all to show up those who are everything" (I Corinthians 1:28 JB). The Lord always seems to choose the despised to carry the Good News of liberation. We may be criticized, but we must not allow that to influence us, for we as gay Christians have a message to proclaim to our own community—"Jesus Christ, the same yesterday, today and forever" (Hebrews 13:8). Therefore let us go forward to do the will of the Lord with confidence and a clear conscience, for we have received the assurance of God's acceptance.

NOTES

1. F. F. Bruce, *Commentary on the Book of Acts* (Grand Rapids: Wm. B. Eerdmans Publishing Co., 1954), reprinted, June 1981 in *The New International Commentary on the New Testament*, pp. 218-19.
2. Luke 2:26-32; Romans 1:17; I Corinthians 1:30.
3. John J. McNeill, S.J., *The Church and the Homosexual* (Kansas City: Sheed, Andrews & McMeel, 1976), pp. 64-65.
4. Donald Goergen, *The Sexual Celibate* (New York: Seabury Press, 1974), pp. 195-96. Copyright © by Donald Goergen. Used by permission of The Seabury Press, Inc.

Part Two
GAY SEXUAL ETHICS

Chapter 9
The Need for Holiness

It has been more than a decade since the beginning of gay Christian religious outreach. It originated with the founding of the Universal Fellowship of Metropolitan Community Churches (UFMCC) and the liberating proclamation that God does accept gay people into the Body of Christ. The phenomenal growth of church-related gay organizations throughout this country and the world is an indication of the gnawing spiritual hunger deep within the souls of many in the gay community. Through the ministry of the UFMCC, through other independent churches such as the Conference of Independent Christians (CIC), and through gay Christian caucuses in some mainline denominations, thousands have come to know the love and acceptance of a personal relationship with Jesus Christ. To this degree, these organizations have indeed been loyal to the propagation of the message of God's loving redemption for all people.

But love's acceptance is not an end in itself. A relationship with the Lord of heaven and earth is one of infinite growth, maturation, and progress, in order that we may become fully conformed to the image of God's unique Son (Romans 8:29). God's acceptance of gay people through that holy love manifested in the redemptive Christ is only a launching pad, as it were, for a journey into the heights of spiritual development to which we have been called by the Lord. However, it is precisely at this stage that the gay Christian movement as a whole faces one of its most important decisions. While it is true that we have a prophetic commission to preach the Good News of God's saving purpose for the gay community, care must nevertheless be exercised not to ignore the twofold command contained in the Great Commission. Not only did our Lord tell his church to "*preach* the Gospel to all creation" (Mark 16:15); he further admonished it to "*teach* . . . them to observe *all* that I commanded you" (Matthew 28:20). While there appears to be an abundance of superficial evangelistic fervor in some gay churches, there seems to be a deficiency in the area of biblical exposition and *in-depth* teaching from the Scriptures. It is becoming increasingly observable that biblical ignorance among gay Christians is not the exception, but the norm. There are numerous gay churches where adult Bible classes are either nonexistent or almost microscopic in size, due to a lack of interest in the Bible and in the way it can relate to our daily activities—a deplorable condition, to say the least.

If the gay Christian community continues to preach only the basic building blocks of "Jesus loves you" and "Gay is good," the growth process into spiritual maturity—understanding *how* to walk with God, as taught in the Scriptures—will surely be stunted. The writer to the early Hebrew Christians chided them for the same laxness in teaching and their lack of hungering desire for the depths of spiritual truth:

> On this subject we have many things to say, and they are difficult to explain because you have grown so slow at understanding. Really, when you should by this time have become masters, you need someone to teach you all over again the elementary principles of interpreting God's oracles; you have gone back to needing milk, and not solid food. Truly, anyone who is still living on milk cannot digest the doctrine of righteousness because he is still a baby. Solid food is for mature men with minds trained by practice to distinguish between good and bad.
>
> Let us leave behind us then all the elementary teaching about Christ and concentrate on its completion, without going over the fundamental doctrines again (Hebrews 5:11–6:1 JB).

A constant diet of "milk" can only prolong spiritual infancy, and the end result, according to the apostolic author, will be a *lack of discernment* between good and evil. Such a condition can be deadly to the gay Christian movement; as the prophet Hosea wrote, "My people are destroyed for lack of knowledge" (Hosea 4:6).

The first section of this book dealt with the fact that grace in their lives operates as an inner witness to believing gay people that God actually accepts them in the context of their sexual uniqueness. The message that gays are under grace, and not under the Old Covenant condemnations of the Law, needs to be proclaimed to all those in the gay community who for too long have labored under the inner guilt engendered by past religious training. However, the provisions of acceptance and forgiveness are not the only implications of God's grace. Just as important is our response to God's love—a willingness to manifest spiritual and sexual responsibility in personal life-style and daily behavior. The apostle Paul cautioned the Christians under his shepherding charge:

> You were called to freedom. . . . Only do not turn your freedom into an opportunity for the flesh, but through love serve one another. . . .
> What shall we say then? Are we to continue in sin that grace might increase? May it never be! . . . What then? Shall we sin because we are not under the law but under grace? May it never be! (Galatians 5:13; Romans 6:1-2, 15 NASV).

Paul was then combating the encroachment into the early church of extreme antinomianism, and it is this same heresy of Live and Let Live! that must be prevented from taking a stranglehold on the spiritual life of the gay Christian community.

Just as the greatest part of the fundamentalist movement within the church has been characterized by rampant homophobia, so in the opposite direction, much of the gay religious community seems to be characterized by an attitude of extremely loose moral permissivism. Unfortunately, some segments of the movement have come from past involvement in the neopagan, hedonistic subculture so prevalent in our society, and they are in a frightful state of ignorance concerning Christian living, a condition a routine weekly sermon cannot even begin to surmount with any degree of success. This is most evident with regard to sexual behavior and/or attitudes relating to morality and life-style. A prime example of the dangers that can arise from a lack of sound biblical teaching has been observed in some of the UFMCC social halls, where it is not uncommon to see displayed, side by side with religious periodicals, advertisements for local baths, bars, and pornographic movies. Some of the early evangelical critics were quick to discern this glaring inconsistency:

> Pornography is a similar issue.... At this point, the gay church is trapped in an uncomfortable situation.... How ought gay Christians to react? We have mentioned earlier some of the incongruities in the congregational newsletters of the Metropolitan Community Church, and the extent of this is indeed startling. Pages filled with articles of praise to God are followed by columns that discuss sexual intimacies; a picture of Christ stands alongside an advertisement for "Diablo's: San Diego's Sin Spot." Equally amazing is the practice of MCC congregations distributing secular gay magazines among its members. In many churches such publications rest alongside Bible study guides and devotional materials.[1]

Perhaps one of the saddest, if not most scandalous examples of the rank carnality that pervades the attitudes and behavior of some members of gay churches can be found in an extremely offensive issue of *The Shepherd's Staff*,[2] the official publication for Good Shepherd Parish Metropolitan Community Church in Chicago. In that particular issue, the "spiritually uplifting" theme was Macho-mania. I am refraining from any direct quotation from the articles, since such excerpts might be considered obscene because of their pornographic explicitness, but it is essential that we be aware of the extent to which some within gay churches have gone in their open acceptance of, and even participation in promiscuous immorality. That issue's spicy variety of "Christian journalism" had a sordidly erotic range indeed. There were the slightly aloof observations of a young man who had made an "academic" tour of a local bathhouse in order to discover the sexual role preferences of those who carry the mystique of the Macho Man in the gay community. However, the objectivity became slightly muddled when the young man himself was willingly seduced. In an even more sleazy vein, another person had written what seemed to be a diary of one night's sexual animalism in and around glory holes and sex palaces, constantly on the prowl for instant sex, usually with anonymous strangers. Throughout the articles, scenes of oral copulation, orgies, and "three-ways" were explicitly described, in one continual escapade of lustful satiation. (If this is truly an outreach of Christian journalism, perhaps I need to reexamine my religious affiliation!)

In the following issue of *The Shepherd's Staff*,[3] there was one letter from a reader who objected to the language and theme of "Macho-mania" as being inappropriate for a religious periodical. However, the pastor of the church, the Reverend Jay Deacon, while apologizing to readers who had been offended by the raw language in that infamous issue, nevertheless defended the publication's refusal to censor such material. He also candidly admitted that there were members of his church who no doubt maintained a life-style similar to that depicted in the "Macho-mania" issue. But the editorial staff was not as conciliatory as their pastor. Stating their conviction that no form of sexual expression can be considered inherently sinful (including the sex described in the previous issue), the editors went on to insist that to graphically relate one's life experiences (presumably including sex) in their church publication is just as important in pointing people to the reality of God as it is to make continual reference to Jesus (?)!

The publication of pornographically oriented literature under the auspices of the UFMCC can only strengthen the basis for allegations made by the anti-gay religious lobbies in Washington, D.C., to the effect that gays are wiping their feet on the morally relevant dictums of sacred Scripture; that the UFMCC is only a church so-called, using clerical collars and the superficial pretense of piety to gain society's acceptance of a life-style consisting of orgiastic sexual abandon.

That kind of writing, when it appears in the official publications of UFMCC churches, or in those of any other group, for that matter, serves as a graphic demonstration of the urgent necessity for gay spiritual leaders to impress upon their parishioners the need for the people of the Lord Jesus Christ to walk in the paths of holy and moral behavior.

> As obedient children, do not be conformed to the former lusts which were yours in your ignorance, but like the Holy One who called you, be holy yourselves also in all your behavior; because it is written, "YOU SHALL BE HOLY, FOR I AM HOLY" (I Peter 1:14-16 NASV).

This brings us, however, to a most important and definitive

question: Just what is the meaning of *holiness* as it relates to the individual Christian's private life-style? More often than not, among rank-and-file church members, the impression tends to linger that holiness is somehow an exclusive property of God's intrinsic, supernatural Otherness, and therefore merely an attribute to be observed in the divine activities of God "out there," holiness being revered only as something totally unattainable for humankind. But the Good News of Jesus Christ, when rightly understood, shatters the myth of God's unapproachableness. Quite to the contrary, the gospel message proclaims God's infusion of the divine nature into the physical, human plane of life.

> For by these He has granted to us His precious and magnificent promises, in order that by them you might become *partakers of the divine nature*, having escaped the corruption that is in the world by lust. Now for this very reason also, applying all diligence, *in your faith supply moral excellence. . . .*
>
> But He disciplines us for our good, *that we may share His holiness* (II Peter 1:4-5; Hebrews 12:10*b* NASV [emphasis mine]).

Holiness, then, can be seen in Sacred Writ as the manifested attribute of the God-nature itself. But by virtue of Christ's redemptive grace, that nature, which is nothing less than the expression of God-ness, can be shared with human beings, thereby transforming them into images of the divine Maker and restoring them to their whole capacity as bodily reflectors of Spirit, an ability that had been lost through the fragmenting effects that resulted from the Fall.

In all this, there is a direct correlation between God's *holiness* and human *wholeness*. The eternal God is totally and self-sufficiently complete in and of God's Self—"I AM ... one God ... who is over all and through all and ... all in all" (Exodus 3:14; Ephesians 4:6; I Corinthians 15:28 NEB). The ultimate expression of God so overwhelms us precisely because it is the supreme manifestation of WHOLE-I-NESS, completeness, fullness of Being: "So may you attain to *fullness of being*, the fullness of God himself" (Ephesians 3:19 NEB [emphasis mine]).

Since the entrance of sin into the cosmos, humanity has lost the ability to adequately reflect the harmonious unity of Deity;

"Hear, O Israel, the Lord our God, the Lord is One" (Deuteronomy 6:4). In our God-rejection, we have entered into a state of spiritual, psychological, and physical *fragmentation*, disunity. Human existence, apart from the healing presence of God through Jesus Christ, can be seen only as a losing and self-destructive battle between our inner divided natures.

> For I know that nothing good lodges in me—in my unspiritual nature, I mean—for though the will to do good is there, the deed is not. The good which I want to do, I fail to do; but what I do is the wrong which is against my will; and if what I do is against my will, clearly it is no longer I who am the agent, but sin that has its lodging in me. . . .
>
> I perceive that there is in my bodily members a different law, fighting against the law that my reason approves and making me a prisoner under the law that is in my members, the law of sin. Miserable creature that I am, who is there to rescue me out of the body doomed to this death? God alone, through Jesus Christ our Lord! (Romans 7:18-25 NEB).

A perfect example can be seen in the instance of sexual lust, in which the fragmentation process of sin creates an imbalance in the interrelationships of one's body, mind, and spirit, to the extent that the body demands pleasurable sensations even against the better judgment of the intellect and/or the loving considerations of one's spirit. This in turn leads to the exploitation of other persons—treating others as mere objects of physical gratification. However, the Good News of Jesus Christ proclaims that it is God's will to integrate the divided aspects of our personhood into one harmonious expression of wholeness: "May God himself, the God of peace, *make you holy in every part*, and keep you sound in spirit, soul and body" (I Thessalonians 5:23 NEB [emphasis mine]). So when we are urged by apostolic injunction to lead *holy* life-styles, we are not being prodded to do the impossible. Rather, we are being called upon to visibly demonstrate the God-nature imparted to us through the Holy Spirit—in every area of our life, whether it be sexual, social, or spiritual. Stressing the role of holiness as the foundation for Christian character, author John R. W. Stott has rightly observed,

Holiness of life, righteousness of character, is then another indispensable mark of the real Christian and of the true church. . . . But if it is God's purpose to make us holy, Satan is resolved to frustrate it. He is seeking ceaselessly both to entice individual Christian believers into sin, and to insinuate evil into the churches. Where he cannot muzzle the church's witness by persecution from without, he resorts to the subtler assault of pollution from within.[4]

And it is precisely this immoral "pollution from within" that will engulf many churches within the gay Christian community, if it is not soon checked by the effective teaching of sound scriptural guidelines.

NOTES

1. Ronald M. Enroth and Gerald E. Jamison, *The Gay Church* (Grand Rapids: Wm. B. Eerdmans Publishing Co., 1974), p. 77. Used by permission.
2. *The Shepherd's Staff*, 2/1 (February-March 1980).
3. *The Shepherd's Staff* 2/2 (April-May 1980), pp. 16-18.
4. John R. W. Stott, *What Christ Thinks of the Church* (Grand Rapids: Wm. B. Eerdmans Publishing Co., 1958), pp. 71-72. Used by permission.

Chapter 10

Sin, Sex, and Scripture:
Life-styles or Licentiousness?

One of the basic problems that underlays much of the "morality paradox" in some gay Christian quarters is the misguided attempt to be what amounts to a projection of the secular homosexual ethos, garbed in religious trappings. In other words, many churches in the gay Christian movement have become merely denominational vehicles by which the ecclesiastical stamp of approval can be put on activities that many in the gay community feel are sexually justified, quite apart from true Christian ethical considerations.

Originally, what has come to be known as the "gay church" was called to be a channel of God's outreach *to* the gay community, most of which has a desperate need for spiritual salvation and inner healing of a sense of lostness and rejection. Accordingly, the mission of the church in the gay community is to proclaim *transformation* through the redemptive process begun when Christ's presence enters the individual heart. Salvation is more than a one-time experience; it is the beginning of the sanctification of the believer, a process of transformation from a state of sin to a life-style permeated with the effects of the Holy Spirit's righteousness. It is a changed way of living, which reflects Jesus Christ in every way possible. *This also includes our sexual conduct.*

Yet, because of trying to stay on good terms with the whole spectrum of gay secular society, many of the religious outreaches have been extremely reluctant to take any stand on these moral issues, since they would be "stepping on people's toes." As a result, much of the mainline gay Christian movement is coming perilously close to receiving the castigation of its Lord: "How can you believe, when you receive glory from one another, and you do not seek the glory that is from the one and only God?" (John 5:44 NASV).

In order not to offend anyone, it appears that some within the UFMCC and other gay religious groups have, in one form or another, attempted to legitimize every life-style popular among gays, no matter how licentious or non-Christian it may be. As one example, the activities at gay baths are being rationalized by numerous persons in the UFMCC as being within the scope of morally permissible forms of Christian sexual expression. In their reasoning, having sex at the baths is not necessarily equated with immoral behavior. James Sandmire, a former elder in the Fellowship, takes this view:

> Paul talks about the freedom of the man who lives in the Spirit. I can't tell you what is wrong. I don't care if you go to the baths. You decide that. If you have the Spirit you are liberated, you can go to the baths, because you don't *have* to go. . . .
>
> You must truly seek relationships—now that can be a one night stand.[1]

Reinforcing this approach is Richard Mickley, past clergyman and an author for the UFMCC:

> Should I go to the steam bath tonight, or should I not go? As controversial as it may sound, there is no law written in heaven which says whether I should or should not go to the steam bath tonight. . . .
>
> There will be variations in the possibilities of love's expression. . . .
>
> Sex should be judged in terms of relationships and not of genital acts. "In this sense promiscuity takes on a different meaning. . . . It should be defined in terms of the quality of the encounter."[2]

Sad to say, this kind of thinking is being perpetrated not merely by an isolated few, but is permeating much of the gay clerical establishment. The following is a typical example:

Not too long ago I was being taken to the airport in one of our cities. Up front, two of the brothers were talking. In the back, a young man I love and respect very much rode beside me. In the middle of an otherwise casual conversation, he handed me a pack of matches advertising one of the local baths, smiled and pointed to himself. I asked if he had enjoyed himself. "Yes," he said "but I was afraid you would think less of me for having been there." I said that I suspected there was often a great deal of lovingkindness at the baths. He remarked that he had seen more acts of Christian charity that night at the baths than he sometimes did in church.

And I suspect that he might be right. I believe that there were probably men there that night—men whom you and I might want to judge—who could have interrupted what they were doing, turned to Jesus Christ and without embarrassment said "Lord, this is a friend of mine." [3]

Those on the bandwagon of this new wave of "liberation theology" have a devious ingenuity for disguising an old heresy with respectability by calling it an alternative Christian life-style. Indeed, from their own words, we have gained valuable insight into the nature of the cover-up. One-night stands have been rationalized into "relationships"; casual sex with strangers has been converted into "acts of Christian charity"; and last but not least, promiscuity's self-justification has been simplified into a nonchalant introduction of one's partner in lust to Jesus! However, all such statements are only forms of verbal subterfuge. Any honest gay male person will readily admit that the main function of the baths is quick, often anonymous genital gratification: corridors of cubicles, with soiled sheets and reclining bodies eager for "hot action"; basement mazes, where naked figures with groping hands hide waiting in shadowy corners; orgy rooms, where groups of men copulate like animals in heat. For those who think this description is overstated, this excerpt from *The Joy of Gay Sex* by authors Silverstein and White should dispel all such suspicions:

> For sheer efficiency, the baths can't be bettered. At the baths making out is certain and more sex can be packed in per hour than anywhere else. . . . In most baths you can take either a locker, which is cheaper, or a room, which is more

expensive. .... The advantage of a room is that it insures privacy for sex. If you don't mind having sex in front of a crowd, then a locker will suffice (you may want to have sex *with* a crowd, and that, too, can be arranged). .... There is public sex, but it occurs only in the dormitories ... the steam rooms or orgy rooms. .... There's a brutal honesty about the baths, but they do serve the interests of pure sensuality.[4]

In reply to this, the Christian Scriptures thunder loud and clear,

Let us behave properly as in the day, not in carousing and drunkenness, *not in sexual promiscuity and sensuality*, not in strife and jealousy. But put on the Lord Jesus Christ, *and make no provision for the flesh in regard to its lusts* (Romans 13:13-14 NASV [emphasis mine]).

When all is said and done, the plain fact is that the issue of the baths is not one of upholding the right to love, but an attempt to gain Christian sanction for the basest expressions of sexual lust.

Some have tried to give spiritual credence to their bath-house escapades by asserting that it gives them an opportunity to "witness for Christ" to the persons with whom they have sex. Ultimately, the logic of this argument would lead us to conclude that the most effective way to witness to prostitutes is by going to bed with them!

There are others who have attempted to claim that the baths are morally acceptable as a sexual outlet because they are perhaps the only opportunity available for the homely, the aged, and the unloved in our community. Sadly, this approach implies a great lack of faith. In light of such an argument, one should ask, with the apostle Paul, "Are you so foolish? Having begun by the Spirit, are you now being perfected by the flesh?" (Galatians 3:3 NASV). Any defense of non-Christian life-styles which encourages spiritually regenerated believers to acquiesce to immorality as the only way out of their personal dilemmas is a direct insinuation that God is not caring enough to bring about "beauty for ashes" (Isaiah 61:3) and total fulfillment in all levels of a Christian's life. When the environment of a gay Christian becomes so desperate that it drives that person to the baths for some fleeting moment of intimate human contact, it becomes an indictment upon the gay church for not providing an atmosphere conducive to finding friendships and relationships outside the ghetto of sleazy bars and baths.

One of the greatest tragedies is that many gay religious leaders have been either afraid or unwilling to expose these demoralizing institutions within their community, choosing instead the path of silence—a muted implication of tacit acceptance. Author Richard Woods brings the issues into sharp focus by adding his criticism of those who refuse to speak out on such critical social dilemmas:

> In every restricted social group, there will be people both eager to be of service and those ready to exploit that limited sphere for everything they can get from it. . . .
>
> Nevertheless, what makes the situation more oppressive and tragic in the [gay] ghetto is that the intermural exploitation of an already socially oppressed minority is being engineered by gays who are only too willing to make a dollar out of the skins of their brethren. . . .
>
> Similarly, in regard to sexual exploitation, it is one thing to disapprove of the baths, beaches and bushes for oneself, but what of others? Keeping *your* head together in a bar with a bad reputation counts for little if your presence there constitutes a tacit recommendation for others. Moreover, your patronization contributes financially to the further exploitation of your gay brothers and sisters.
>
> Even creating alternatives to the dehumanizing sexual circuses of the baths and other concrete forms of exploitation will accomplish little if the existence of such establishments continues without any kind of resistance or criticism.[5]

Most important of all, the argument that seeks to justify the baths as a last resort for the lonely and sexually needy is an approach that runs counter to the admonition of the One who shows us the way, Jesus Christ:

> That is why I am telling you not to worry about your life and what you are to eat, nor about your body and how you are to clothe it. . . . Can any of you, for all his worrying, add one single cubit to his span of life? And why worry about clothing? Think of the flowers growing in the fields; they never have to work or spin; yet I assure you that not even

Solomon in all his regalia was robed like one of these. Now if that is how God clothes the grass in the field which is there today and thrown into the furnace tomorrow, will he not much more look after you, you men of little faith? So do not worry; do not say, "What are we to eat? What are we to drink? How are we to be clothed?" It is the pagans who set their hearts on all these things. Your heavenly Father knows you need them all. Set your hearts on his kingdom first, and on his righteousness, *and all these other things* [food, clothing, and other personal needs] will be given you as well. So do not worry about tomorrow: tomorrow will take care of itself. Each day has enough trouble of its own (Matthew 6:25, 27-34, JB [emphasis mine]).

If we consistently apply our Lord's teaching from his Sermon on the Mount, we can see that the anxiety about lack of companionship that drives one to forms of depersonalized sexual expression, whether it be at the baths or at a brothel, is an indication of an unhealthy negative preoccupation with one's needs—that faith in God's providence has given way to fear of unfulfillment. Jesus says that God already knows our deepest needs and that rather than being overly anxious about them, we should focus on earnestly seeking the kingdom of God and his will for our lives. Jesus promised that God will certainly meet our most pressing needs—including our need for love and intimate relationship. But the moment we take matters into our own hands in an attempt at fulfillment of our desires through a compromise in moral standards and behavior, we automatically identify ourselves as faithless and unbelieving.

The widespread acceptance of bath-house sexuality is yet another indication that biblical standards of holiness and sexual purity are virtually nonexistent in numerous gay congregations. On this and other subjects, some Christian gays are resorting to a form of intellectual sophistry, complete with theological double talk, instead of turning to the New Testament Scriptures for basic guidance and teaching. "Every divinely inspired scripture is also useful for the teaching of the truth, for the refutation of error, *for moral correction*, and for training in the good life" (II Timothy 3:16 Barclay [emphasis mine]).

At this point,there are no doubt those who feel that I seem to be reversing my earlier perspective on the importance of Scripture. It might appear that while I minimized the application of biblical injunctions against homosexual acts, I now seem to be doing an about-face, emphasizing the centrality of the New Testament's guidelines with reference to sexual behavior. Such perceptions, however, are due in large part to a lack of understanding as to which areas are, and which are not the proper spheres of scriptural authority. For example, many of the apostolic writings which made reference to certain forms of homosexual activity were written from an existential standpoint; their authors were totally unaware of the scientific and psychological realities that make up the complexity of sexual orientation. Therefore, for one to use such writings as the ultimate authority on how we should view homosexuality, irrespective of the scientific evidence, would be tantamount to insisting that we should adhere to the Ptolemaic system of astronomy simply because of its great antiquity and because the holy prophets and saints of old, such as Joshua, subscribed to it (Joshua 10:12-13). So we see that those areas of scientific and/or sociological discovery that were unknown to the biblical authors—whether they concern the heavens or homosexuality—certainly cannot properly qualify as being under the jurisdiction of scriptural authority.

On the other hand, the question of immoral sexual expression has nothing to do with the issue of sexual orientation, a predisposition over which the individual has little or no control. Sexual morality involves the conscious and deliberate choice of expressing one's sexuality in a way that conforms to the spiritual guidelines for personal conduct given in the New Testament. To the apostolic authors, the central core of sexual immorality revolved around the sins of adultery, prostitution, and casual promiscuity—and for good reason.

Adultery is not some kind of ancient taboo that modern society has suddenly outgrown. The emotional carnage due to adultery has been strewn about our nation in the form of broken marriages; bewildered and deserted children, innocent pawns in the tragic chess of marital deception; tragic breakdown in people's ability to trust; and devastated expectations of fidelity in personal relationships.

Sexual promiscuity has little more to commend it to the moral sensibilities of a Christian culture. That irresponsible game of hopscotch through bedrooms has gone a long way toward creating an American subculture whose priorities are pleasure at any price and lust-obsessed body worship.

In light of these considerations, it is most appropriate, if not essential, that we place our principal emphasis upon the guidelines for sexual relationships found in the Christian Scriptures. They are not archaic; neither are they outdated. If anything, they are just as contemporary in their answer to the destructive effects of the freewheeling sexual anarchy of the "new" morality as they were almost two thousand years ago, when the same forms of permissiveness were in vogue. Some will contend that because these sexual advisements are directed toward heterosexuals, they therefore have no application for gay relationships. But this accusation is not valid, for there are no double standards—one for gay and one for non-gay. Sexual immorality is not determined by the gender of those involved, but by the moral values that strengthen and uphold the sanctity of human relationships. And for the seeking, committed Christian, whether liberal or conservative, these values can most properly be discerned through the filter of the scriptural authors who attempted, to the best of their ability, to glean the mind of the Spirit who inspired them.

It is only too obvious that some in positions of leadership among gay Christians (primarily those of the UFMCC) need to take more seriously their calling as shepherds of the flock of God under their care by being more responsive to the Holy Spirit through the reproving and correcting ministry of scriptural counsel. It is little wonder that many of them are woefully inadequate in their ability to teach a biblically sound approach to a Christ-becoming holy life-style, when they themselves are often hesitant to act as examples of spiritually responsible moral behavior. However, the members of a congregation should never pervert the need for their pastor to provide an exemplary model into an excuse to set up impossible double standards, projecting upon the minister an obligation of moral perfection from which they consider themselves exempt. There is no room for such disparity of conduct among those who seek to follow the pattern of the New Testament Church; we are *all* priests of the New Covenant, called upon to offer not only the sacrifice of praise (I Peter 2:5), but also the sacrifice of our bodies, that in all things *(including our sexual life-styles)*, we may reflect in our actions the purity to which Christians have been called:

> So then, brothers, I urge you by the mercies of God *to offer your bodies to God as a living, consecrated sacrifice*, which will delight God's heart, for that is the only worship which a rational being can offer God. *Stop always trying to adjust your life to the world's ways.* You must get a new attitude to life; your whole mental outlook must be radically altered, so that you will be able to decide what God's will is, and to know what is good and pleasing to him, and perfect (Romans 12:1-2 Barclay [emphasis mine]).

As the apostle makes clear, the believer's worship is not confined to the mouthings of liturgical phrases on Sunday morning. Worship and thanksgiving to God are also expressed in the way we relate to one another with our physical selves, for we are to honor God with our bodies (I Corinthians 6:20). Paul, in one of his earliest Epistles, again piercingly zeroes in on a Christian's sexual conduct, and how it should differ from that of nonbelievers:

> You know what instructions we gave you by the authority of the Lord Jesus.
>
> It is God's will that you should be holy; *that you should avoid sexual immorality; that each of you should learn to control his own body in a way that is holy and honorable, not in passionate lust like the heathen,* who do not know God; and that in this matter no one should wrong his brother or take advantage of him. The Lord will punish men for all such sins, as we have already told you and warned you. *For God did not call us to be impure, but to live a holy life.* Therefore, he who rejects this instruction does not reject man but God, who gives you his Holy Spirit (I Thessalonians 4:2-8 NIV [emphasis mine]).

Sin is an unpopular word in some quarters of the gay religious community. The subjects of immorality, sexual impurity, and lust are equally taboo as pulpit topics. People generally do not wish to hear anything that tends to disturb them or make them uncomfortable, especially if it involves coming to grips with those scripturally undesirable life-styles to which their lower natures cling with such tenacity. But the simple truth is clear:

> Those who live on the level of our lower nature have their outlook formed by it, and that spells death; but those who live on the level of the spirit have the spiritual outlook, and that is life and peace. For the outlook of the lower nature is enmity with God; it is not subject to the law of God; indeed it cannot be; *those who live on such a level cannot possibly please God. . . .*
>
> So sin must no longer reign in your mortal body, exacting obedience to the body's desires (Romans 8:5-8; 6:12 NEB [emphasis mine]).

Unless this advice is heeded, much of the organized Christian gay experience will eventually fulfill the prophetic apostasy.

> For the time will come when they will not endure sound doctrine; but wanting to have their ears tickled, they will accumulate for themselves teachers in accordance to their own desires; and will turn away their ears from the truth, and will turn aside to myths. (II Timothy 4:3-4 NASV).

Yet, true to human nature, there seems to be a strong tendency among many in the gay Christian movement to simply dismiss examples of indecent behavior as being merely amoral "alternative life-styles," optionally viable for the gay believer and not necessarily having any negative effect upon spirituality!

This author has also heard some in gay clerical circles argue that a sexually promiscuous life-style is merely a symptom of a deeper problem, or disorder, to which our primary attention should be focused. It is very true that there often are times when people become deeply entangled in the web of obsessive promiscuity because of low self-esteem and an overriding craving for acceptance and love. Psychologists have long been aware of this phenomenon. Usually, in such cases, when people are brought to understand their inherent self-worth through therapy, they no longer find themselves in need of constant reaffirmation of their personhood through a merry-go-round of shallow sexual encounters.

However, to use this argument as the general explanation for the high percentage of those in the gay community who maintain a life-style characterized by promiscuity is to give it an overstated application. There are many who have not been psychologically driven to promiscuity. Quite the contrary, their participation in a loose life-style has been freely chosen because they *enjoy* it. There are, unfortunately, numerous gays who crave the continual excitement of new and different sexual escapades nightly, who continually lust for the sensuous pleasures of unrestrained orgies.

Taking all this into consideration, it is time gay ministers stopped making excuses for their parishioners who are so entrenched in the carnality of illicit sex that they are unwilling to give up such practices. Many gay clergy do not want to deal with the uncomfortable necessity of meeting "head on" the many "symptoms" that make up the bulk of the male gay community's life-style.

A parallel can be seen in the case of a person plagued with a common headache. Now, while it is true that the headache is in all probability a physical symptom of inner mental tension and stress, this does not mean that the person will refuse to treat the headache pain by taking an aspirin! So also with the symptoms of sub-Christian sexuality (whatever the varied causes may be). We cannot do less than follow the example of Jesus, who, when confronted with the woman who had been taken in adultery, began at that very moment to minister to the root of her problem with love and forgiveness, thereby showing the woman her worth before God. But Jesus did not ignore the outer symptoms, which manifested themselves in her acts of adultery; instead, he acknowledged her behavior and ordered the remedy: "*Go, and sin no more*" (John 8:1-11 [emphasis mine]).

The general feeling of many nominal members of the UFMCC, as well as those of other gay churches, is that the current life-styles in our homophile community are acceptable to the church as long as the individuals involved act toward others in a way that does not "hurt" them (their interpretation of *hurt* is extremely vague). This positional stance results in only meager disapproval, from numerous gay pastors, of constant bed hopping, park cruising, the bath scene, and even abusive sadomasochism. In fact, the "tricking syndrome" is a permanent fixture in the lives of many gay Christians, usually because their leadership has rarely pointed them toward the revelation that Christ has opened up to them the freedom to be themselves, apart from bondage to sexual idolatry.

The common excuse-all line of reasoning used by many is that as long as there is mutual consent, and neither partner is "hurt" physically or emotionally, sexual activity cannot be considered sinful. This argument fails on two counts. First, what is or is not sinful (basically, to *sin* is to miss the mark of God's perfect plan for one's life) is determined by divine revelation, not by personal opinion. Second, the Scriptures give a very definitive description of sin: "Anyone who sins at all breaks the law, because to sin is to break the law" (I John 3:4 JB). What law?—"the life-giving law of the Spirit" (Romans 8:2, NEB). The NASV translation succinctly renders I John 3:4*b* as "Sin is lawlessness."

It is truly unfortunate that many today confuse our liberty in Christ with some form of spiritual anarchy in which we are free to do anything we please, or anything we consider right, based solely on our own opinion. The holy writers of old stated otherwise: "There is a way which seems right to a man, but its end is the way of death" (Proverbs 14:12 NASV). To repeat, *sin* is simply missing the bull's eye of the target that God has set up for our life's purpose. From our limited human perspective, what actually is a sinful course of action may often seem to be the right thing to do. But the apostle Paul reaffirmed the ancient proverb, "The wages of sin is death" (Romans 6:23).

A perfect example is found in the Old Testament book of Judges, in which an era of Israel's early history, full of bloodshed, degeneracy, and lack of direction, was vividly portrayed. The reason for such a despairing national condition is given in the last verse of the book: "In those days there was no king in Israel; everyone did what was right in his own eyes" (Judges 21:25). Like the Israelites during that disruptive time, many Christians in the gay community seem to be unaware that they *do* have a King— One who presently reigns over the church—and that One is none other than Jesus Christ himself. As a result of their inability to perceive his Lordship over their lives and the relevance of his commandments given in Scripture, they are following instead a circular road in a spiritual wilderness, where their own opinions become signposts to disaster.

The notion that if a person's sexual expressions constitute a "gay life-style," they are somehow morally acceptable is flatly contradicted time and again throughout the New Testament. Many gays have often heard from the pulpits of their own churches that they must never reject any who come into their midst simply because their life-style is different or not fully understood. This usually culminates in a plea to accept, therefore, all the varied life-styles within the confines of the gay subculture. This line of reasoning has one grave defect: It contradicts the basic apostolic admonitions of our faith. While it is true that Jesus affirmed repeatedly that *"whosoever will* may come" (Revelation 22:17 [emphasis mine]), and that no one who comes to him will be cast away (John 6:37), nevertheless, it was that same Jesus who pointedly told his disciples that those who, after several warnings, flagrantly continued in a life-style of sin were to be put out of the local congregation (Matthew 18:15-18). And this procedure was reinforced by Paul in his writings (II Thessalonians 3:6, 14-15).

At this point, some readers are no doubt thinking, "What right do you have to pass judgment on other people's actions? After all, Jesus said that we weren't to sit in judgment of others!" It is truly unfortunate that the act of *judging*, or the quality of being *judgmental*, has taken on such a negative connotation in today's society. This stems in part from a general misunderstanding of Jesus' words, "Do not judge, lest you be judged." From a cursory reading, many assume that our Lord was preaching against *all* forms of judgment upon others. But this is not the case; in the very next verse, he continues: "For *in the way you judge*, you will be judged; *and by your standard of measure*, it shall be measured to you" (Matthew 7:1-2 NASV [emphasis mine]). In a recent book, evangelical author Peg Rankin made this pertinent observation:

Do we have a right to judge another person's spiritual condition? . . .

A Scripture passage that is often quoted out of context is the first verse of the seventh chapter of Matthew. It reads, "Judge not, that ye be not judged." How many times is it quoted in a lifetime to cover all kinds of situations? Actually, it is not a universal statement; it was never meant to apply to every situation. In fact, Christ goes on to mention two situations in which it must not apply. The first occurs in verse 6. He says, "Give not that which is holy unto the dogs, neither cast ye your pearls before swine, lest they trample them under their feet, and turn again and rend you." In order to distinguish a pig from a sheep, we have to make a judgment. Otherwise, we may be spiritually torn to pieces.

The second situation occurs in verse 15: "Beware of false prophets, which come to you in sheep's clothing, but inwardly they are ravening wolves." How do we tell a false prophet without making a judgment?

The answer is we can't.[6]

In context, then, it is evident that Christ did not forbid us to exercise judgment on persons and/or situations, but was calling us to *responsible* judgment. As a matter of fact, Jesus actually *commands* us to judge: "Do not keep judging according to appearances; *let your judgment be according to what is right*" (John 7:24 JB [emphasis mine]). The NASV translates this last phrase as "Judge righteous judgment." Once again, we see that Scripture simply reinforces two important principles:

1. We are not to judge others by our own prejudice, ignorance, or superficial assumptions.
2. We *are* encouraged to judge fairly and intelligently, and only in accordance with the compassion of Christ and the commandments of God.

As Christians, we are instructed not to judge unbelievers by our own spiritual and moral standards, since those persons are not part of the church. However, as members of the Body of Christ, we are commanded to make definitive and discerning judgments regarding any morally offensive and publically known behavior of those who claim the name of Jesus. If their life-styles contradict their claim, they thereby bring reproach to the church and to the holiness of Christ for which it stands. Yet such judgment is not to be founded only upon personal opinion; it should be determined and formulated by the basic truths and guidelines contained in the Christian Scriptures. Paul's explanation of this position is both plain and to the point:

When I wrote in my letter to you not to associate with people living immoral lives, I was not meaning to include all the people in the world who are sexually immoral, any more than I meant to include all usurers and swindlers or idol-worshippers. To do that, you would have to withdraw from the world altogether. What I wrote was that you should not associate with a brother Christian who is . . . a usurer, or idolatrous, or a slanderer, or a drunkard, or is dishonest; you should not even eat a meal with people like that. *It is not my business to pass judgment on those outside. Of those who are inside [the church], you can surely be the judges.* But of those who are outside, God is the judge.

You must drive out this evil-doer from among you (I Corinthians 5:9-13 JB [first emphasis mine]).

This chapter is not a tirade directed against the secular gay community at large, for as Paul said, God is its judge. However, when we join the Community of Christ, we put ourselves under the rule of the teachings and moral correctives of the Christian faith. When people continue to call themselves Christian while they persist in living like pagans, it should not be tolerated. In such cases, it is imperative that the properly constituted authorities in the churches take appropriate action, including judgment-evaluation of members' *publically* known behavior that is deemed an affront to the standards of Christ and sound apostolic teaching. The church has every right to exercise both judgment and official discipline upon habitual offenders.

This does not mean, however, that the church should arrogate unto itself an inquisition-type attitude, which could easily encourage the rise of malicious church "gestapo squads," anxious to pry and peek into people's private lives. The church can legitimately deal only with situations that are commonly known within the local congregation, such as the case of the man who was living incestuously with his stepmother (I Corinthians 5:1-2). What Christians do in the secrecy of their private lives, whether sinful or wholesome, is between themselves and the discerning scrutiny of God's judgment; it is not the province of the church to be unhealthily preoccupied with bringing to light the hidden things of darkness which the Lord has declared to be his exclusive sphere of administration (I Corinthians 4:5).

As to the wholesale acceptance of any and all life-styles currently popular in the gay community—the Bible gives us one yardstick by which we may determine whether they are fitting for one who professes Jesus Christ: *A life-style should conform to the guidelines contained in the New Testament Scriptures.* On this subject, the Scriptures have much to say:

Try, then, to imitate God . . . and follow Christ by loving as
he loved you. . . . *Among you there must be not even a mention of fornication or impurity in any of its forms, or promiscuity: this would hardly become the saints! . . . For you
can be quite certain that nobody who actually indulges in
fornication or impurity or promiscuity—which is worship-
ping a false god—can inherit anything of the kingdom of
God. Do not let anyone deceive you with empty arguments; it
is for this loose living that God's anger comes down on those
who rebel against him.* Make sure that you are not included
with them. . . .

You spent quite long enough in the past living the sort
of life that pagans live, behaving indecently, giving way to
your passions, drinking all the time, having wild parties and
drunken orgies and degrading yourselves by following false
gods (Ephesians 5:1-8; I Peter 4:3 JB [emphasis mine]).

Obviously, this catalog of life-styles does not contain any that
would be acceptable for the Christian believer, whether homosexual or heterosexual. As a matter of fact, in the passages just quoted,
the apostle Paul equated such loose sexual conduct with idolatry.
This is not hard to understand, for most forms of promiscuity are
manifestations of the obsessive worship of sensual gratification. In
other words, sexual conquest and the ecstasy of orgasm have become the gods of the promiscuous, to the detriment of any hope
for progress in a walk with God. Those who are intent on having
sex only for the sake of sex, merely using other people in the
process, are no better than unbelievers, and their portion will no
doubt be with the hypocrites. In light of these passages from the
Scriptures, it is hard to believe that someone who has credentials
of ministry from the UFMCC could pen the following words:

Should you "trick"; should you act out your S&M fantasies;
should you be involved in "orgies"; should you be living in
an open relationship or a monogamous one? I cannot say. I
can speak to only what works for me, and offer ideas that
have helped me. The decisions you choose to make are
yours. What is *ethical* or *moral* for me may not seem so to
you. What you do or do not do may seem *unethical* to
me—but that, too, is a part of assuming responsibility for
our own lives and actions.[7]

This kind of thinking is nothing but moral relativism—the humanistic philosophy which asserts that there are no moral Absolutes, that there is no ultimate Truth—no black and white, but only "shades of gray." It is the antithesis of the biblical Christian revelation that reveals Truth in the person of Jesus Christ himself (John 14:6) and in the Words the Father gave him to speak—those pertaining to conduct, as well as to doctrine (John 8:31-32; 12:47-50). And indeed, Jesus certainly *did* have something to say about our sexual life-styles:

> That which proceeds out of the man, that is what defiles the man.
>
> For from within, out of the heart of men, proceed the evil thoughts and *fornications* (i.e. *acts of sexual immorality* [marginal reading]), thefts, murders, *adulteries*, deeds of coveting and wickedness, as well as deceit, *sensuality*, envy, slander, pride and foolishness. All these evil things proceed from within and defile the man (Mark 7:20-23 NASV [emphasis mine]).

Immorality is not determined by our own opinions, nor is Christian morality the product of our private intellectual creation. Rather, moral conduct is that which is in accord with the Words and will of the living Christ; immoral conduct is that which violates the commands and guidelines given us by the Lord:

> "Why do you call Me, Lord, Lord, and do not do what I say? ... The one who has heard [my words], and has not acted accordingly, is like a man who built a house upon the ground without any foundation; and the torrent burst against it and immediately it collapsed, and the ruin of that house was great...."
>
> "If anyone hears My sayings, and does not keep them, I do not judge him.... He who rejects Me, and does not receive My sayings, has one who judges him; *the word I spoke is what will judge him at the last day*" (Luke 6:46,49; John 12:47,48 NASV [emphasis mine]).

In his teaching, Jesus made it quite clear that there are forms of sexual expression that are immoral and evil. "If it feels good, do it!" has no place in the canon of Christian proverbs. There has long been a popular myth circulating in the gay Christian community—a myth implying that Jesus said nothing critical about homosexual expression. This assumption can be very misleading, for as we have already observed, in the seventh chapter of Mark, Jesus unequivocally condemned *any* form of sexual expression (whether homosexual or heterosexual) that is devoid of fidelity (i.e., adultery) or commitment (i.e., promiscuity). This, of course, eliminates any possibility of Christian sanction for orgies, open relationships, and the general milieu of promiscuous eroticism. No matter how cleverly certain self-styled theologians attempt to veil the corrupting spirit of lust with the verbal cloak of "alternative life-style" or "liberation from outworn, archaic standards," the holy Scriptures will stand as an open rebuke, a testimony against such perversion of the Gospels' directives.

> But false prophets also arose among the people, *just as there will also be false teachers among you*, who will secretly introduce destructive heresies . . . *promising them freedom while they themselves are slaves of corruption* (II Peter 2:1,19 NASV [emphasis mine]).

It is plainly evident, in light of the quotations which already have been presented from supposedly devout clergy in the service of God, that false teachers who advocate the libertine doctrine of sexual "freedom" have infiltrated the gay church in fulfillment of this prophetic prediction. Even The Reverend Troy Perry, one of the pioneers of the gay Christian movement and founder of the UFMCC, has stated his support for such pernicious teachings:

> I believe that there can be loving experiences, even in a one-night stand. I truly believe that two individuals can meet and share their complete beings with each other, totally sexually too, and never see each other again; and remember it as a beautiful, loving situation.[8]

J. Harold Greenlee, an outspoken critic of the gay cause, has made some penetrating observations with regard to Perry's statement:

> If such promiscuous one-night stands of homosexual activity would have God's approval, then surely he would approve of similar heterosexual encounters. But these God

condemns as fornication and adultery! How then can we presume to claim God's approval of such an encounter in a homosexual relationship? ... Nor do the defenders of homosexual behavior argue to legitimize only settled relationships. They do not reject promiscuous homosexual behavior. Instead, they argue for their right to casual relationships. What they insist on is complete freedom for any type of same-sex acts and behavior, without restraint.[9]

I am proud to announce that this is one gay Christian apologist who does *not* so argue! Greenlee's point is well taken. Too often in their defense of their sexual expression, many gays have gone to the extreme of arguing for the green light on just about all forms of homosexual activity, making no distinction between that which is constructive and moral and that which is immoral and depersonalizing. Any attempt to turn the casual encounter of a one-night stand into a momentary "meaningful relationship" betrays an unholy desire to twist the plain intent of Jesus' teaching—to whitewash his condemnation of lustful promiscuity and infidelity.

The almost infinitesimal amount of concern shown in the gay Christian community over the plague of promiscuity which envelopes a large percentage of its members is ample indication that the Lordship of Jesus Christ is not being taken seriously as it applies to our private life-styles. Following in the footsteps and teachings of Christ may not be easy, but that does not excuse us from making an effort at obedience.

Some individuals regard sexual permissiveness as a basic human freedom. For the Christian, it is a question of liberty or lordship. Freedom is only meaningful in terms of the specific purpose it serves. . . . If sexual freedom means freedom to violate God's appointed order, it is not a God-given freedom but merely an individual's independent choice. Freedom in Christ is a precious gift, but it is not freedom to be irresponsible. . . . Freedom to be promiscuous means one is no longer free to fulfill God's purpose. Freedom to fulfill God's purpose is no longer freedom to be promiscuous. In other words, one freedom cancels out the other. For Christians, the true freedom is to obey the highest command, to fulfill the highest purpose, to escape the destructive, defeating consequences of freedom's abuse. . . .

The law of love is not a substitute for the moral law, but a summary and a fulfillment of it. Thus when the Scriptures speak again and again against fornication and adultery— against every manner of sexual sin—the obedient Christian will heed that word as his response of love to God.[10]

The gay Christian movement cannot continue to ignore this issue without losing its credibility as an authentic approach to devout discipleship. Our church services may resound with the echoes of liturgical praise for Jesus, but if our sexual behavior is in direct contradiction to his teachings, we then become living testimonials to our rejection of him as Lord. In the words of Jesus,

You hypocrites, rightly did Isaiah prophesy of you, saying,

"THIS PEOPLE HONORS ME WITH THEIR LIPS,

BUT THEIR HEART IS FAR AWAY FROM ME.

BUT IN VAIN DO THEY WORSHIP ME,

TEACHING AS DOCTRINES THE PRECEPTS OF MEN" (Matthew 15:7-9 NASV).

Our sexuality can become an aspect of our discipleship, or a reflection of our degeneracy. We can honor the Lord with our lips only, or with our lives. The choice is ours.

NOTES

1. Quoted in Ronald M. Enroth and Gerald E. Jamison, *The Gay Church* (Grand Rapids: Wm. B. Eerdmans Publishing Co., 1974) pp. 77-78. Used by permission.
2. Richard R. Mickley, *Christian Sexuality* (Los Angeles: Universal Fellowship Press, 1976), pp. 156, 166, partially quoted from Deane Ferm, *Responsible Sexuality Now* (New York: The Seabury Press, 1971), p. 127.
3. Joseph Gilbert, "Lord, This is a Friend of Mine . . . ," *The Gay Christian* (October 1977), p. 7.
4. Charles Silverstein and Edmund White, *The Joy of Gay Sex* (New York: Simon & Shuster, 1977), pp. 20-21. Copyright © by Mitchell Beazly Publishers Ltd. Used by permission of Crown Publishers, Inc.
5. Richard Woods, *Another Kind of Love: Homosexuality and Spirituality* (Chicago: Thomas More Press, 1977), pp. 126-28. © The Thomas More Press by Richard Woods. Reprinted with permission.
6. Peg Rankin, *Yet Will I Trust Him* (Glendale, Calif.: Regal Books, G/L Publications, 1980), p. 106.
7. Pepper Shields, "Toward A Sexual Ethic," *In Unity* (June/July 1980), p. 27.

8. Troy Perry, quoted by Harvey N. Chinn, *Texas Methodist/United Methodist Reporter* (March 14, 1975), from Charles Lerrigo, "MCC: The Church Comes Out," *New World Outlook* (May 1973).

9. J. Harold Greenlee, "The New Testament and Homosexuality," in *What You Should Know About Homosexuality*, ed. Charles W. Keysor, (Grand Rapids: Zondervan Publishing House, 1979), pp. 87-88. Copyright © 1979 by The Zondervan Corporation.

10. Dwight Harvey Small, *Your Marriage is God's Affair* (Old Tappan, N.J.: Power Books, Fleming H. Revell Co., 1979), pp. 119, 121. Copyright © 1979 by Dwight Harvey Small. Used by permission.

Chapter 11
Open Relationships

ertain publications of the Universal Fellowship of Metropolitan Community Churches, such as the book *Gay
Lifestyles* by Anglican process theologian Norman Pittenger, have gone so far as to argue that a nonmonogamous, "open"
relationship should be considered a morally sanctioned form of
Christian life-style. It is often argued by the proponents of open
relationships that such sexual nonexclusivity is actually a liberating experience, and as such can be an avenue for greater
emotional growth and maturity for a couple, as long as such an
arrangement is acceptable to both individuals. This is the essence
of Pittenger's reasoning. In fact, he even has the audacity to assert
that in order to insure a lasting love relationship, both persons
should be allowed the freedom to engage in occasional sexual
contact with others:

> I believe that one of the conditions for a genuinely success-
> ful union is the allowance of a degree of freedom for the
> partners, so that the union [gay relationship] will not be
> threatened when there are such [sexual] contacts, "passing
> fancies" as someone has put it; but accepted precisely be-
> cause it is understood in advance that homosexual unions
> are not identical with the expectations usually found in
> conventional heterosexual marriage. . . .
>
> It may very well be the case that now and again a loyal
> partner in a gay union will engage in what I have styled an
> occasional contact—for fun, because of affection or liking,

as a way of manifesting friendship, or . . . simply because of "plain lust" or urgent and irrepressible sexual desire. . . . But if this is understood, accepted, seen as part of life (so to say), there is little likelihood that the primary union will be broken up.[1]

However, the best biblical ethics do not agree with Norman Pittenger. Written in the context of warnings against the folly of unfaithfulness and adultery, here is some sage advice, and its meaning is unmistakable:

Drink the waters from your own cistern, fresh water from your own well.
Do not let your fountains flow to waste elsewhere,
nor your streams in the public streets.
Let them be for yourself alone,
not for strangers at the same time.
And may your fountain-head be blessed!

Find joy with the wife you married in your youth,
fair as a hind, graceful as a fawn.
Let hers be the company you keep,
hers the breasts that ever fill you with delight,
hers the love that ever holds you captive.
Why be seduced, my son, by an alien woman,
and fondle the breast of a woman who is a stranger?
(Proverbs 5:15-20 JB)

In regard to the giving in to momentary sexual desires, the apostle Peter had this to say; "Beloved, I urge you as aliens and strangers *to abstain from fleshly lusts, which wage war against the soul*" (I Peter 2:11 NASV [emphasis mine]). The apostle John went even further: Any person who allows him or herself to be dominated by "passing fancies," cannot be walking under the influence of the love of God:

You must not love this passing world
or anything that is in the world.
The love of the Father cannot be
in any man who loves the world,
because nothing the world has to offer
—the sensual body,

the lustful eye,
pride in possessions—
could ever come from the Father
but only from the world;
and the world, with all it craves for,
is coming to an end;
but anyone who does the will of God
remains for ever (I John 2:15-17 JB).

So we see that a continual lustful craving for illicit sensuality, and any life-style that encourages such behavior in a Christian's walk, is to be rejected for what it is—the direct antithesis of apostolic guidelines for holy, balanced, Christian sexual expression.

In his whole section on the subject of fidelity, Pittenger makes two serious mistakes. First, he intimates that since it is an increasingly common practice for husbands, wives, and lovers to have "occasional contacts" outside the relationship, we must therefore be realistic Christians and at least have a moderate tolerance for such practices![2] But lust, no matter how prevalent in society, must never be accepted, or even tolerated by true Christians, for as Peter stated, lust wages *war* against our souls. One channel through which our lower nature can destroy the effectiveness of our spiritual walk with God is through the undermining of our discipline over our sexual selves, which can lead only to moral degeneracy. The tragedy that resulted from David's lust for Bathsheba is ample witness to its destructive potential (II Samuel 11, 12).

Second, Pittenger says that the "closed character" of marriage is in reality a *negative* aspect of this sacred institution![3] He attempts to reinforce his point by quoting from *Open Marriage* by George and Nena O'Neill, which propounds the same permissive philosophy with regard to heterosexual relationships:

Fidelity in the closed marriage is the measure of *limited* love, *diminished* growth and *conditional* trust. This fixation in the end defeats its own purposes, encouraging deception, sowing the seeds of mistrust and limiting the growth of both partners and so of the love between them....

Fidelity then is redefined.... It is loyalty and faithfulness to growth, to integrity of self and respect for the other, not to a sexual and psychological bondage to each other....

New possibilities for additional relationships exist, and open (as opposed to limited) love can expand to include others ... beside[s] your mate.[4]

Pittenger and those he appeals to for support are advocating nothing short of *consensual adultery!*

"Let marriage [an ongoing, one-to-one, sexually committed relationship] be held in honor among all, *and let the marriage bed be undefiled*; for fornicators and adulterers God will judge" (Hebrews 13:4 NASV [emphasis mine]). To commit adultery is literally to *adulterate*, or *dilute*, those relational bonds of sexual intimacy and fidelity which God intended to be unique for two lovers alone. What Pittenger recommends in his disturbing literary contribution on the subject of gay life-styles can serve only to perpetuate the plague of promiscuity, which infects our community through so-called open relationships.

It is truly pathetic to see this noted scholar following in the path of the religious scribes whom Jesus sternly accused of neglecting the commandments of God in order to observe their own cleverly devised opinions (Mark 7:8). In *Gay Lifestyles*, Norman Pittenger has sought to so totally ignore or reinterpret the commandment "You shall not commit adultery" (Exodus 20:14) that its force as a molding influence upon sexual morality becomes minimal, at most. However, for those who wish the simplicity of truth, the implications of the commandment still stand as an abiding testimony to God's perfect will for the sanctity and purity of human sexual expression.

As for the contention that open relationships add richness, variety, and a liberating dynamic often missed within the "limiting strictures" of monogamy, one has only to read the conclusions of a woman whose journey through the maze of swinging life-styles led her to realize, on purely *nonreligious* ground, the ultimate superiority of a monogamous relationship.

In an article titled "Viva Monogamy!" appearing in *Forum* magazine, Lisa Davis related that she had long bought the hedonistic myth that monogamy would guarantee erotic monotony and mediocrity.[5] One man (she thought) was not enough. But, her thinking has undergone a significant shift toward an appreciation for the monogamous ideal, in that it is not merely more socially acceptable than the sexually permissive life-style; it is also the most *advantageous* arrangement for the accentuation of personal growth. Davis goes on to list the numerous interpersonal "pluses" inherent in monogamy, including a spiraling sense of deepening intimacy (as opposed to a superficial physical closeness scattered among many casual lovers). Not to be overlooked is the richness and variety of a sexually uninhibited monogamous union, which explores and expresses the constantly changing emotions of the couple in strengthening their psychic interaction through new heights of ecstasy. Monogamy is therefore a means of solidifying one's sense of personal identity and relational stability in a socially chaotic society where sex has become an end in itself.

This same point of view has been endorsed from a religious perspective by a former elder of the UFMCC, who offers at least six reasons for the superiority of a monogamous relationship. He concludes:

> It is my personal conviction that a monogamous (on-going, one-to-one) condition is the more perfect way to express a relationship. ... There is an old saying that "the grass is always greener on the other side of the fence." Certainly there will be attractive individuals that will be observed and encountered ... some may even offer an opportunity ... but, if one already has a lover relationship, it is by far the best to avoid those temptations and allow the ultimate expression of love, the sex act and other intimate activities, to be reserved for only the beloved mate. If one reserves self for only the chosen partner, only good can come from it. ... A union of two souls working as one in God is in the perfect Will of God. ... God created it. ... God blesses it.[6]

Some gay advocates of sexual permissiveness raise the objection that gay unions or relationships cannot be compared to and, indeed, should not be patterned on heterosexual marriage covenants in terms of exclusivity or ethics. But such an argument is like a bucket full of holes—it can't hold water. It would, in effect, set up a double standard—one for homosexuals and another for heterosexuals. The qualities essential to the growth and continuance of a relationship—love, loyalty, faithfulness, commitment—do not change simply because of a couple's sexual orientation. Ironically, the arguments in support of the playboy philosophy among heterosexuals are nearly identical to those in favor of gay hedonism: freedom from "Victorian" rules of behavior, liberation to explore one's sexuality, and so on. As we have seen, Norman Pittenger bases much of his liberal approach to gay ethics upon the controversial *Open Marriage*, which seeks to justify "relaxed" morality within the heterosexual community.

Conversely, the reasons advanced for the validity and attractiveness of exclusive monogamy are virtually the same for both heterosexual and gay couples, with one major exception: gay unions, unlike marriages, are not recognized under the law. Yet it is important to realize that the lack of a legal document to officially confirm one's relationship is no excuse for setting aside standards and expectations, especially the Christian tenet of monogamous commitment for the nurturing of mutual love.

The concept of open relationships is nothing new. It had its origins in the patriarchal institution of polygamy—that degrading practice which used women primarily as sex objects and baby machines. They were treated as chattel and often retained or discarded according to male whim. So today, under the guise of "openness," the old polygamous desire for new varieties of sexual conquest has reared its ugly head within the realm of homosexual life-styles, encouraged by the "sexual supermarket" atmosphere prevalent in certain parts of the gay community. Many gays, especially males, have become erotically spoiled. Sex is cheap, if not free for the asking. Such ingrained promiscuous habits are hard for many to give up, and as a result, the popularity of the open arrangement has increased. Numerous gay couples have become too lazy to work at building and strengthening a monogamous relationship, choosing instead the easy way of minimal commitment to insure that they do not totally lose their "freedom to explore." When a couple makes it known that they have an open arrangement, it amounts to little more than an attempt to add a verbal veneer of respectability to the continuation of mutual hedonism and lust.

To be sure, there *are* biblical instances of open, three-way (or more properly, triangular) relationships. Abraham, Sarah, and Hagar present a fitting example (Genesis 16). Yet the Bible records the result: the jealousy of Sarah, Hagar's hardship, heartbreak, and rejection, and the perplexity of Abraham, an individual truly caught in the middle! Although the Scriptures make note of the fact that some of the ancient patriarchs practiced varying forms of nonmonogamous relationships, this does not serve as a divine commendation of the practice. It must be taken into account that the Old Testament is a record of cultural living patterns *as they were*, not necessarily *as they should have been*, in light of God's original and perfect plan. Nowhere does the Bible command polygamous or open relationships. It is true that polygamy was tolerated under the Old Covenant (Deuteronomy 21:15ff.); it was nevertheless discouraged for those in positions of leadership who were to be examples for the rest of the nation (Deuteronomy 17:17).

For those who advocate nonmonogamous agreements between lovers because they crave a casual variety of sexual partners, Solomon is an excellent case in point. With his 700 wives and 300 concubines, it is fair to assume that sexual boredom was not one of his problems! But the final results of his hedonistic dissipation were idolatry, a broken and damaged relationship with the Lord, and the loss of part of his kingdom (I Kings 11:1-14).

Finally, the assumption that "we should not invest monogamy with the sacred significance of being the only legitimate Christian . . . form of familial structure," as one UFMCC publication has propounded, runs counter to the whole of New Testament teaching on the subject![7] *No records of the early church, either in the Gospels or the Epistles, show any sanction whatsoever for nonmonogamous convenantal relationships being in the perfect will of God.* Confirmation of this can be found in the Edenic ideal, which was clearly based on monogamy (Genesis 2:20-25), and upon which the Lord Jesus put his seal of approval (Matthew 19:1-9). In fact, the first mention of polygamy in the Bible is in Genesis 4:19, 23-24, where such a departure from the norm of God's intent was attributed to the wicked Lamech, of the line of the murderous Cain.

When we examine the New Testament, it becomes evident that if one is serious about following apostolic advice in regard to open relationships, it can be easily found. While admittedly, there is not a specific command against the practice of polygamy, there is a strong inference that nonmonogamous relationships are decidedly sub-Christian and improper for a believer. In I Timothy 3:2, Paul put forth a list of qualifications he considered essential for a Christian leader. The fact that the spiritual overseers of the church were to be examples of godly behavior (I Peter 5:3) indicates that the quality of life-style required of those in ministry was expected also of the rank and file of the faithful. Near the top of Paul's list in I Timothy was the requirement that the man deemed appropriate for the spiritual office of leadership must be "faithful to his one wife" (NEB). In an exposition on this verse, biblical commentator Albert Barnes has made some pertinent comments on the implications of this requirement. He too believes that the prohibition of polygamy among the ecclesiastical leadership was for the express purpose of setting a higher moral example for the congregations, pointing them back to God's original plan for sexually monogamous commitment.[8]

We find that in the first-century society of Paul's era, not only was polygamy lawful, but sexual unfaithfulness was widespread, especially among the Gentiles.[9] Cultural practices during the days of the early church were not entirely unlike some of the emerging social/sexual practices of our own day. In the time of Paul, polygamy was one legal means by which a man could insure his permanent access to sexual-partner diversity. Today's increasing trend toward open marriage and/or open relationships is accomplishing the same goal, as modern society moves more and more toward permissive life-styles permeated with the mores of sexual nonexclusivity. So we see that whether one places the emphasis of the command in I Timothy upon sexual faithfulness, or upon the charge to have only one wife, the implications are obvious. In the words of one perceptive commentator, "The import is plain: the bishop must be free of any suspicion of loose sexual relationships." [10] And if we are to approach this topic with any degree of moral honesty, we must frankly admit that open relationships are precisely that—"loose sexual relationships."

Putting the heterosexual context of the passage aside for the moment, it is plain that among the early Christians, the only kind of sexual relationship considered to be God-glorifying was a union between two people, each of whom was faithful to the other *exclusively*. Therefore, if we wish to measure our sexual life-styles by authentic Christian guidelines and principles, there can be no room in our viable options for open relationships. The choice is ours: We can live like the pagan Gentiles, whose adherence to sexual faithfulness was virtually nonexistent, or we can follow the apostle's admonition to stand out in contrast to a corrupt society through our allegiance to the commitment of sexual responsibility, following the divinely ordained monogamous ideal.

NOTES

1. Norman Pittenger, *Gay Lifestyles* (Los Angeles: Universal Fellowship Press, 1977), pp. 109-10, 112.
2. Ibid., pp. 109-10.
3. Ibid., p. 105.
4. Nena O'Neill and George O'Neill, *Open Marriage*, (New York: M. Evans, 1972), pp. 256-57. Copyright © by Nena O'Neill and George O'Neill. Reprinted by permission of the publisher, M. Evans & Co., New York, NY 10017.
5. Lisa Davis, "Viva Monogamy!" *Forum* (November 1979), pp. 47-50.
6. Richard C. Vincent, "Relationships: An Opinion," *New Life* (a Christian outreach of MCC-LA) (May 1975), p. 8.
7. Richard R. Mickley, *Christian Sexuality* (Los Angeles: Universal Fellowship Press, 1976), p. 98.
8. Albert Barnes, *Barnes' Notes on the New Testament* (Grand Rapids: Kregel Publications, Edited by Ingram Cobbin. First American Reprint Edition 1962. Reprinted in 1963, 1966, 1968, 1970, 1972, 1974, 1975, 1976, 1978, & 1980), p. 1139.
9. *The Broadman Bible Commentary* (Nashville: Broadman Press, 1971), vol. 11, p. 317.
10. Eric Lane Titus, "The First Letter of Paul to Timothy," in *The Interpreter's One-Volume Commentary on the Bible*, ed. Charles M. Laymon (Nashville: Abingdon Press, 1971), p. 886.

Chapter **12**

A Biblical Approach to Balanced Sexuality

The writers of the Bible—of the New Testament, in particular— were by no means antisexual; they were however, against the *degradation* of genuine Christian expressions of human sexuality. There is a misconception being popularized by numerous liberal theologians, to the effect that the apostle Paul was antisexual.[1] On the contrary, Paul encouraged the development of healthy sexual expression between husbands and wives. In fact, he was extremely leery of sexual abstinence in a couple's relationship, except for the purpose of prayer:

> Let the husband fulfill his [sexual] duty to his wife, and likewise also the wife to her husband. The wife does not have authority over her own body, but the husband does; and likewise also the husband does not have authority over his own body, but the wife does. Stop depriving one another, except by agreement for a time that you may devote yourselves to prayer, and come together again lest Satan tempt you because of your lack of self-control (I Corinthians 7:3-5, NASV).

Paul's preference for the state of chastity was determined primarily by his expectations that the Second Coming of Christ was imminent; therefore he felt an urgent need to propagate the gospel before the approaching end. Family life was not expedient to the fulfillment of Paul's calling as an apostle, but in no way could his outlook have been considered antisexual.

While the Bible is careful never to divinize sex, as did the ancient fertility cults, neither does it go to the opposite extreme. It never treats sex as merely another form of physical appetite to be satisfied whenever and with whomever the urge arises. From such a standpoint, sexuality would become only a vehicle for the satisfaction of the senses. Paul dealt a lethal blow to such a pagan-influenced philosophy when he roundly scolded the early Christians at Corinth, a city known through much of the ancient world as the pleasure center of the Roman Empire. At that point, Corinth's low standards were beginning to influence its Christian inhabitants, and to this Paul addressed himself directly:

> "There is nothing which I may not do," you say. I quite agree, but it is not everything whose results make it worth doing. "There is nothing which I may not do," you say. I quite agree, *but there is nothing by which I will allow myself to be dominated.* "Food is for the stomach," you say, "and the stomach for food." True, but the day will come when God will destroy both the stomach and the food. *The body was never meant for fornication;* it was meant for the Lord, and the Lord for the body. . . .
>
> Are you not aware that our bodies are parts of Christ? And am I then going to take the limbs which rightly belong to Christ and make them the limbs which belong to a prostitute? God forbid! You must be well aware that, if a man joins himself to a prostitute, he becomes physically one with her. For as scripture says: "These two shall become one person." But if a man joins himself to the Lord, he becomes spiritually one with him. *Have nothing to do with fornication.* Every other sin which a man may commit is outside his body, but the fornicator sins against his own body. Are you not aware that your body is the temple of the Holy Spirit, who dwells within us, and whom we have received from God, and that you therefore do not belong to yourselves? He bought you for himself—and it did not cost him nothing. *Therefore honor God with your body* (I Corinthians 6:12-20 Barclay [emphasis mine]).

The root meaning of *fornication* in the Greek is *prostitution,* but this does not refer only to professional prostitution. Unfortunately, many sexual encounters in our gay community are little more than a prostitution of personhood, a game of masks where super-ficial beauty is sold for a fleeting sense of acceptance. Yet all the while, that deep yearning for *authentic* love screams out for fulfill-ment in the inner recesses of the heart.

We know, of course, that the New Testament authors under-stood certain forms of sexual expression to be definitely outside the pale of responsible Christian morality. Throughout their writ-ings, we find Christ and his apostles repeatedly condemning acts of adultery and fornication.

The meaning of *adultery* is obvious to most, but many gay people are perplexed as to the meaning of *fornication*. Exactly what constitutes an act of fornication? Probably the most accurate way to explain *fornication* so that it can reasonably be applied to present-day circumstances is to remove it from the heavily stric-tured, traditional explanation, which is too blanketing a generalization. According to the tenets of Christian orthodoxy, fornication has been defined as any kind of sexual activity outside the institution of heterosexual marriage. But there is no flexibility in such an archaic definition to help gay Christians solve their own problems of personal morality. Our definition must be inclusive enough to encompass the entire spectrum of heterosexual, bisex-ual, and homosexual orientations. Therefore we must adopt the simplest, most basic ethic that will adequately reflect the biblical intentions with regard to wholesome sexual relationships.

There are several valid approaches to sexual morality within the larger Christian community which differ noticeably, in certain fine-line areas, as to exactly when or under what circumstances sexual activity can be said to have, in fact, crossed over into im-moral or unconstructive behavior. It is not my intention to pursue those various approaches in detail, for there are other more schol-arly works which have quite adequately covered their diverse perspectives, and these should certainly be investigated by the in-terested reader.[2] However, I feel the simplest interpretation is that, according to the overall premise of the New Testament, responsi-ble sexual expression ideally should be rooted within the confines of love and commitment. That does *not* mean love *or* commit-ment—it necessitates the presence of *both*. Two persons will hard-ly commit themselves to an enduring relationship if there is no love between them. Similarly, that which some call love cannot be truly so if it does not issue from a mutual willingness to relational commitment. Today there are many who will not hesitate to declare their "love" for another in an aggressive, not-too-subtle attempt to bed a partner for an evening. But when the morning light dispells the mists of the previous night's illusions, most have awakened to the sad realization that those crooning moans of "love" were no more than the thinly veiled pantings of lust.

Unfortunately, the single (and searching) gay person is often faced with the dilemma of being virtually unable to meet other eligible gay people apart from an atmosphere such as that in bars, baths, and other less reputable establishments, which overtly encourages casual promiscuity. And, we have seen, more often than not, gay churches have contributed to these limited options by encouraging the patronization of such businesses. The church in the gay community could go a long way toward improving the situation by stressing the need for courtship prior to sexual intimacy. Courtship is very often overlooked as a way of getting to know another individual in the wholeness of his or her personhood. It is a wise and socially accepted avenue of exploring the possibility of relationship-compatibility, at the same time guaranteeing mutual respect and integrity and thus avoiding the pitfall of depersonalized promiscuity.

One of the most negative characteristics of frequent "tricking" with strangers or new acquaintances is the inability to express actual love for another's totality as a unique human being. It is impossible for sex with a person one has just met to be a thoroughly fulfilling and genuine expression of love. One cannot love someone one does not know. At most, such sex is a response to first impressions and body chemistry. This illustrates part of the difficulty that is encountered, especially in the gay community, in discovering the proper, divinely ordained function and meaning of sex. Far too often, gay persons, caught up on the whirling merry-go-round of one-night stands, have fallen into the habit of using sex as a means of introduction to a new-found acquaintance. But intimacy should be initiated only between those whose feelings have drawn them together in a developing relationship of loving commitment.

Any expression of interpersonal sexuality apart from the bonds of love, or lacking even the *intention* of seeking or strengthening a committed relationship, is seen from the biblical perspective as a denial of the Creator's original intent; and it is seen in the New

Testament as yet another form of irresponsible sexuality. The wording of this last statement is careful and deliberate, in order to avoid a sweeping condemnation of all sexual behavior between single persons. This was done for good reason. While it is clear from the apostolic witness that casual, promiscuous sex is ruled out as a fitting practice for the Christian, there are, nevertheless, certain circumstances which seem to remove sexual activity between single people from the classification of mere hedonistic recreation—for instance, couples engaged to be married or those who have been dating for an extended period of time.

Actually, the roots for this leeway in tolerance are to be found in some of the ambiguities and silences of the Bible itself. Generally speaking, one cannot always appeal to the Old Testament for good examples of culturally acceptable moral behavior. However, a mental note should be made that with reference to premarital sex, the Hebrew Scriptures are surprisingly less dogmatic than many have been led to assume. With regard to these areas of leniency, one historical researcher took pains to stress that there is no

> ban on pre-martial sex; it is seldom appreciated that nowhere in the Old Testament is there any prohibition of non-commercial unpremeditated fornication—apart from rape, and subject to the father's right to claim a cash interest in a virgin.[3]

Walter Wink, professor of biblical interpretation at Auburn Theological Seminary, has also written in confirmation of this fact:

> The Bible nowhere explicitly prohibits sexual relations between unmarried consenting adults—a discovery that caused John Calvin no little astonishment. The Song of Songs eulogizes a love affair between two unmarried persons, though even some scholars have conspired to cover up the fact with heavy layers of allegorical interpretation.[4]

From this, we can assume the Hebrew culture's acknowledgment of certain forms of sexual expression not technically within the parameters of official wedlock, but sanctioned as permissible, by virtue of the absence of any restrictions in the Law. This is relevant for us, since that same silent ambiguity is carried over into the New Testament, by virtue of the types of sexual circumstances that were never formally addressed.

We have no record of specific words from Jesus on the matter [of premarital sex], though the basic value of human dignity in sexual relations is utterly clear in his thought. Paul's vigorous condemnation of prostitution seems to represent for him every form of depersonalized sexual activity, but the *porneia* he censured was not clearly directed at premarital intercourse as such. . . . In short, the Bible assists us with general perspectives but not with specific injunctions. If the Old Testament is specific about the sexual violation of property rights and about idolatrous and cultic intercourse, and if the New Testament is specific about prostitution, adultery, and incest, neither gives highly concrete guidance on premarital sex—even though their basic theological perspectives are perennially relevant.[5]

The word that is often translated in the Epistles as *fornication* cannot, in and of itself, prove a blanket condemnation of *all* forms of sexual activity outside of marriage, as is often implied by traditionalists. Originally the word *porneia* primarily signified prostitution, and the majority of its occurrences in Paul's letters probably refer to that ancient institutional vice, as I Corinthians 6:12-20 seems to corroborate; but with the passage of time, *porneia* also came to be associated with certain other forms of socially reprehensible behavior.

At times in the New Testament (Acts 15:20, 29; 21:25; 1 Corinthians 5:1ff), the word is used to prohibit marriage within the degrees of kinship forbidden by the Old Testament (Leviticus 18:6-18). Elsewhere (1 Corinthians 6:9; Galatians 5:19; Ephesians 5:5; Colossians 3:5; Hebrew 13:4; Apocalypse 2:14), the condemnation referred to intercourse with prostitutes. In each of these instances, however, the Greek *porneia* was translated into the Latin vulgate as *fornicatio*, a translation which led many to interpret the New Testament condemnation of prostitution as including all forms of premarital sexual intercourse. . . .

Catholic moralists today recognize that the condemnation of *porneia* in the New Testament refers variously to adultery, incest, and the depersonalization and promiscuity exemplified by prostitution. There is no prohibition of all premarital intercourse as such. . . . It does not address the question of loving, responsible sexual intercourse of a couple engaged to be married.[6]

This means that we are liberated from any kind of overly moral legalism which insists that sexual activity between two people in love is always considered sinful unless first blessed by some kind of holy union ceremony. The scriptural data simply does not warrant such puritanical rigidity. The chief value of the apostolic condemnations of fornication lie in their affirmation of the concept that sex is meant to be purposeful and creative in terms of strengthening relational cohesivity; any sexual expression which denies or falls short of that divine expectation must be rejected as unwholesome.

For the gay Christian, the sex act should no longer be seen as simply a pleasurable way to obtain satisfaction of a physical appetite; even animals do that by instinct! It is to be hoped that we have progressed beyond that point in our moral perceptions. Conceiving of one's sexuality as an intimate secret, within which is contained the highest physical revelation of one's selfhood, waiting to be unconditionally released as a gift to the beloved partner, can go a long way toward encouraging one to contemplate the special fulfillment of sexuality in a closed relationship. This is due in part to its elevation of the sexual act to exemplify the sensual zenith of human love, giving, and intimacy.

But when sexual activity is used merely as a means to communicate casual friendship, there remains no other more intimate physical way in which love can be expressed to the one who has come to be considered as infinitely more than a friend. Sex then loses its special secrecy as a totally private pleasure; densensitizing us to the uniqueness of sex-in-relationship as intended by love's Creator.

To be sure, there are some questions that do not have easy answers. When can one be certain that one is in a committed relationship? Does such a relationship commence with an actual ceremony and an "I do" at the altar, or does it begin with the conversational exchange of feelings, goals, fears, and hopes for the future? At just what point is sexual expression both appropriate and needful between two people who feel attraction and love, but have not yet "formalized" a commitment? Is sex to serve not only as the supreme compliment issuing forth from commitment, but as a confirmational witness that such a commitment should be finalized, due to compatibility on all three planes—physical, emotional, and spiritual? Perhaps the best answers to these questions can be gained only through attempting to view things in light of God's perspective as we ask the Holy Spirit for insight.

God created us as sexual beings, not only for the purpose of procreation, but also to enable us to relate to each other in an intimate way that would make possible the expression of Love's essence and divinity in a physical act of human sharing. Most of the biblical passages dealing with sexual relationships were originally intended for situations involving heterosexuals. However, in reading the Scriptures, it becomes rather easy to apply many of those same guidelines to a current, constructive blueprint for the development of gay Christian relationships.

Many people have assumed that in order to live as a Christian, one must give up the basic pleasures of life, but this attitude shows a misunderstanding of God's plan that we should live as *balanced* individuals.

> Go, eat your bread with joy
> and drink your wine with a glad heart;
> for what you do God has approved beforehand.
> Wear white all the time [a symbol of joyous living],
> do not stint your head of oil [an invitation to the 'good life'].
> Spend your life with the woman [or lover] you love, through all the fleeting days of the life that God has given you under the sun; for this is the lot assigned to you in life and in the efforts you exert under the sun (Ecclesiastes 9:7-9 JB).

God never intended that people should intentionally deprive themselves of all the good things that were originally created to be enjoyed—including human sexuality. Christ himself has told us, "I came that they might have life, and might have it *abundantly*" (John 10:10b NASV [emphasis mine]). Paul wrote, "Everything created by God is good, and nothing is to be rejected, if it is received with gratitude" (I Timothy 4:4 NASV). As gay Christians, we should thankfully accept our sexuality as a gift through which we may express the joyousness of our love for another. In fact, all through the Scriptures, metaphors of sexual union and/or marriage are used to illustrate not only God's tender love for Israel, but Christ's love for his church. One has only to read from a modern translation of the Song of Songs to see that the attraction between two lovers becomes a beautiful parable, illustrating the Lord's yearning for humanity to be united with God in close and loving union. It also makes plain that physical sensuality is not foreign to the Bible as an appropriate and healthy expression of intimacy, within the God-ordained context of loving and committed relationship.

Sex, used properly, is indeed a blessing from the Lord, but when it is abused, it can become a *curse*. When Christians make an idol of sex by giving it first priority, even placing it above the commandments of our Lord Jesus Christ, it becomes an expression of sin, for they are "serving the creature rather than the Creator" (Romans 1:25). If there is anything to which the gay Christian community must take heed, it is the final admonition of the apostle John in his first Epistle: "Little children, guard yourselves from idols" (I John 5:21). Since we live in a sophisticated and technologically advanced society, it is a common mistake to assume such a warning to be anachronistic, for certainly, it is argued, we no longer worship sculptured images of stone! Literally, perhaps not. But many still worship what those idols originally symbolized, and this is especially true (though certainly not exclusively) in the gay community.

> You shall not make for yourselves idols, nor shall you set up for yourselves an image or a *sacred pillar* . . . for I am the LORD your God. . . . you shall not worship their gods, nor serve them, nor do according to their deeds, but you shall utterly overthrow them, *and break their sacred pillars in pieces* (Leviticus 26:1; Exodus 23:24 NASV [emphasis mine]).

The cultures and nations driven by Israel from the land of promise were zealous devotees of Canaanite fertility religions, which venerated sacred pillars. These pillars, according to scholars, were nothing less than symbols of *an erect penis*. They were usually situated on high hills and in groves of trees, along with images known as Asherim, representing female fertility; and they were always popular during the times of Israel's apostasy from the Lord (I Kings 14:22-24).

One of the greatest problems within the Christian gay fellowship is the general lack of willingness to "break in pieces" the sacred pillars of sexual idolatry—the lustful obsession which becomes a primary force in determining the course of one's life-style when not under the dominion of the Holy Spirit's guidance. The prophet Joel counsels us to "rend your heart, and not your garments" (Joel 2:13). In other words, the outer garments of superficial piety are not enough; it is the shrines of personal idolatry in the depths of our hearts which must be completely torn down if the Spirit of Christ is to sit enthroned as our total Lord.

In this whole sexual controversy, it must be realized that the New Testament Scriptures draw a distinction between legitimate sexual activity, which can be both life enhancing and dynamic, and the illicit, erotic behavior which externalizes destructive psychological preoccupations. It *does* differentiate between love and lust. The holy Scriptures *do* have a positive attitude toward sex as God intended it to be expressed. However, as we have seen, there *are* areas of sexual expression which are condemned in no uncertain terms as being a violation of the godly principles which affect our development into the perfected image of Jesus Christ. In our walk with God, we gay believers cannot afford to ignore the guidelines for humanizing relationship, founded on the love and wisdom of Christ.

NOTES

1. Many persons have accused Paul unjustly of being antisexual because of a statement mistakenly attributed to him, to the effect that it is good for a man not to touch a woman. However, William Barclay's translation goes a long way toward correcting this unfortunate assumption by making it plain that the statement did not originate with Paul, but was made by those in Corinth who were questioning Paul on such matters: "With reference to the contents of your letter, and in particular in regard *to the point you make* that it is an excellent thing for a man to have nothing to do with women, my verdict is this . . ." (I Corinthians 7:1 [emphasis mine]).

2. Anthony Kosnik et al., *Human Sexuality: New Directions in American Catholic Thought* (New York: Paulist Press, 1977), pp. 152-69. ©1977 by The Catholic Theological Society of America. Used by permission of Paulist Press.

3. G. Rattray Taylor, *Sex in History* (Harper & Row; New York: 1954, 1970), p. 241.

4. Walter Wink, "Biblical Perspectives on Homosexuality," *The Christian Century* (November 7, 1979), p. 1083. Copyright 1979 Christian Century Foundation. Reprinted by permission.

5 *Embodiment: An Approach to Sexuality and Christian Theology* (Minneapolis: Augsburg Publishing House, 1978), pp. 153, 188.

6. Kosnik et al., *Human Sexuality*, pp. 24, 155.

Chapter 13

The Upward Call of Christ: A Challenge for Change

There is much more at issue here than the failure of the gay Christian outreach to accurately expound upon the entire body of Scripture in order to instruct gay believers in the proper Christian life-style. Far more chilling is the horrifying possibility that ultrapermissive sanctions for carte-blanche sexuality will prepare the way for the eventual crystalization of such ideas into a mold similar to that of the first-century apostasy spoken of by Jude:

> My friends, I was fully engaged in writing to you about our salvation . . . when it became urgently necessary to write at once and appeal to you to join the struggle in defence of the faith. . . . It is in danger from certain persons who have wormed their way in. . . . They are the enemies of religion; *they pervert the free favour of our God into licentiousness. . . .*
>
> They follow their lusts. Big words come rolling from their lips. . . .
>
> [They are] worldly minded, devoid of the Spirit [NASV].
>
> . . . There are others for whom your pity must be mixed with fear; hate the very clothing that is contaminated with sensuality (Jude 3-4, 16*b*, 19, 23 NEB [emphasis mine]).

Referring to the same group of sensualist heretics, our risen and glorified Lord, in his visionary unveiling to John on the island of

Patmos, issued a warning to the Universal Church that he would *declare war* on any heresy which taught the people of God a permissive countenance of sexual lust and impurity.

To the angel of the church at Pergamum write:

"These are the words of the One who has the sharp two-edged sword: . . . I have a few matters to bring against you: you have in Pergamum some that hold to the teaching of Balaam, who taught Balak to put temptation in the way of the Israelites. He encouraged them to eat food sacrificed to idols and to commit fornication, and in the same way you also have some who hold the doctrine of the Nicolaitans. So repent! If you do not, I shall come to you soon and make war upon them with the sword that comes out of my mouth. Hear, you who have ears to hear, what the Spirit says to the churches!" . . .

To the angel of the church at Thyatira write:

"These are the words of the Son of God. . . . I have this against you: you tolerate that Jezebel, the woman who claims to be a prophetess, who by her teaching lures my servants into fornication and into eating food sacrificed to idols. I have given her time to repent, but she refuses to repent of her fornication. So I will throw her on to a bed of pain, and plunge her lovers into terrible suffering, unless they forswear what she is doing; and her children I will strike dead. This will teach all the churches that I am the searcher of men's hearts and thoughts, and that I will reward each one of you according to his deeds" (Revelation 2:12, 14-17a, 18, 20-24 NEB).

The condition of the early church was not always solidified and monolithic. During the latter part of the first century, many of the churches were rent apart over the issue of Gnostic doctrines. The Gnostics held that they had been initiated into the "higher mysteries" of the faith, which supposedly were unknown to the common lot of believers. Many denied that Jesus had become incarnate in human flesh. It was this teaching, known also as Docetism, which was vehemently attacked by the apostle John in his Epistles. Most Gnostic doctrine was based upon the premise that all matter is evil. Hence, from that standpoint, anything physical as a vehicle for the Incarnation would have been beneath the dignity of God. Therefore many Gnostics insisted that Jesus had had only some form of phantom body.

There were different sects among the Gnostics, but there seem to have been two mainstreams of thought stemming from the premise that evil is implicit in the material universe. One group was primarily characterized by a rigorous asceticism which sought to deny the body all pleasures of the flesh. Its members refused to drink wine, maintained a frugal diet, and some denied the wholesomeness of sexuality, even within the marriage bond (I Timothy 4:3). Paul argued extensively against this school of Gnosticism in his Epistle to the Colossians.

On the other end of the heretical spectrum were the Gnostic libertines. They, too, devalued the worth of the physical body, but quite in contrast to the ascetics, they believed that the spirit is the only valuable part of a human being in relation to spiritual progress; therefore what one does with one's body is inconsequential and irrelevant. This viewpoint sometimes went so far as to stress that indulgence in sexual promiscuity and pleasures of the flesh could not hamper spiritual growth, since God is concerned only with perfection of the spirit.[1]

These Gnostics taught that the physical body could not be redeemed and was doomed to destruction. For this reason, many denied the concept of bodily resurrection (I Corinthians 15:12). Apparently, some encouraged extremes of pagan licentiousness as a way of exploring "the deep things of Satan" (Revelation 2:24) and thereby discovering the shallowness of the pleasures of the physical world as compared to the ecstasy of the spirit's illumination when freed from the material realm of the senses. It is this heresy of spiritual libertinism which Christ so savagely castigated in the book of Revelation.

The resurrection of Jesus Christ demonstrates that redemption is to be total—for the *whole* person, body, soul, and spirit (I Thessalonians 5:23). Therefore, what we do with our bodies is vitally important, for the personal theology of the New Testament is decidedly *incarnational*. Through the miracle of regeneration, we reflect in different degrees the incarnate manifestation of the Holy Spirit within. "Do you not know that your body is a shrine of the indwelling Holy Spirit? ... Then honour God in your body" (I Corinthians 6:19-20 NEB).

The Christ who speaks to the church in the passage from

Revelation is far removed from the popular image of "gentle Jesus, meek and mild." Here we are confronted by an angry Lord who has no tolerance for sexual immorality or any life-style that would compromise his clear commands to single-hearted discipleship. It is therefore imperative that those segments of Christ's Church with an outreach in the gay community not openly or officially tolerate licentious sexuality in the Body of Christ. Otherwise, they risk inciting the furious, holy anger of the Lord Jesus Christ.

> "Just a little idolatry," they [the Gnostic libertines] murmured. "Just a little immorality. We are free. We do not have to go to extremes." Such blatant reasoning is sometimes heard in the churches today. "A man must have his fling," it is said. "It is no use being idealistic. We are all human, you know. Christ does not expect too much from us. His demands are not unreasonable. He knows we are dust." Totally different is Christ's view of this matter. . . . Christ calls the church to . . . repent of its error and its evil, for He is deeply concerned about a church which is tainted with such things.[2]

Nor will reliance on the record of gay accomplishments in other aspects of Christian activities aid in averting the judgment of God upon the gay church movement for its hesitance or its outright refusal to present to the people the *full* implications of living the gospel.

The modern manifestation of sexual libertinism within the gay church is not based upon the same philosophical premise as that of the early Gnostics, but the end result in terms of immoral behavior is the same. The Gnostics denigrated the physical as being unworthy of the spiritual. The modern libertines in the gay church, on the other hand, celebrate the physically sensuous as a gift from God, supposing that the expression of a natural gift, such as sex, can only enhance the development of a person's total sense of bodily acceptance. This form of reasoning is insidiously deceptive, in that it contains a large enough kernel of truth to make it appealingly acceptable to the spiritually unlearned. Indeed, our sexuality should be celebrated as a gift from God. But the gift was not accompanied by a blank check. The teachings of our Lord are strikingly clear on this matter, as his anger with the church over the tolerance of sexual promiscuity among its members quite forcibly demonstrates. As some in our midst move closer and closer to becoming modern manifestations of the ancient Balaamite heresy, they will stand out in the annals of heaven as the greatest betrayers of the gay community, for they will have been instrumental in teaching "another gospel" (Galatians 1:9), a gospel which provides no higher vision for the gay Christian experience than a continuance in the person-degrading mire of purposeless sexual abandon.

It is sadly ironic to see many gays who have actually been deceived into believing that this hedonism is somehow indicative of their liberation from heterosexual society's oppression. This seems to be the thrust of John Rechy's notorious literary composite *The Sexual Outlaw*. However, nothing could be further from the truth. The anonymity of bath-house encounters, the dark shadows of alleyway bars, and the camouflage of city park shrubbery—all were the products of a society that forced gay people into secretive, seedy, morally corrupt life-styles.

But now, precisely because we *have* made decisive strides toward liberation from self-loathing and a greater acceptance in society (though the struggle is far from complete), we no longer need be forced to fulfill the promiscuous roles which in the past were imposed upon us by heterosexual establishment restrictions. We are now free to form a leisurely courtship, rather than seek a hurried pick-up for the night. Some of us are even free to make a public declaration of our settled relationships. We are now free to take time to relate to one another as *whole* gay persons, cultivating our spiritual and emotional as well as physical closeness.

If our fellowship is to be a true expression of gay *Christian* liberation, we must have the courage to emerge from the shell of shallow sexuality which heterosexual prejudice has decreed to be at the core of the gay community's corporate identity. As followers of Jesus Christ, we have been called to rise above the stereotypes projected of us, and to reflect instead the "whole-i-ness" of love, which includes our sexuality as an integrated part of the Christian self-expression.

The heresy of sexual libertinism poses a peril to the gay Christian community also because of the price it exacts from our physical well-being. The plague of promiscuity, which has infected the gay community at large, has created a venereal disease epidemic of massive proportions. New and bizarre strains which are predominantly unique to the gay community are being detected and have alarmingly defied the ability of medical research to find cures. Commenting on this dangerous and unexpected development, a recent editorial in *The Advocate*, America's national gay news magazine, brought the point forcibly home in its blunt and realistic manner:

> So terrifying is the spread of the new illnesses in our community that even those august journals of Establishment myopia, *Newsweek* and the *New York Times*, have found them newsworthy. . . .
>
> Whether we like it or not, the fact is that aspects of the urban gay lifestyle we have created in the last decade are hazardous to our health. The evidence is overwhelming. . . .
>
> Those gay men who behave as if they were the only people on the planet and whose sole purpose in life is to get their rocks off, even when they are diseased, are a threat to us all. . . .
>
> One thing is abundantly clear. Those of us who remain unconscious about our sexual behavior are playing Russian roulette with our health and our lives. If we pay little heed to the consequences of having sex, every fuck is another pull of the trigger. Our lifestyle can become an elaborate suicidal ritual. Our safety and survival depend on each of us and our individual behavior.[3]

The concern for spiritual and sexual responsibility being felt by some of the more sober-minded within the gay Christian movement is not to be construed as a call for the implementation of restrictive regulations designed to give gay churches an appearance of more "respectability" or bind them to the shackles of pharisaical self-righteousness.

Nor should this book be taken as a legalistic manifesto, smugly decreeing what is and is not a violation of Christian ethics. It is rather a cry against the many forms of self-destructive sexuality which only succeed in entrenching the psyche-fragmenting effects of impersonalness, alienation, lust, and erotic obsession. The Apostle Paul strongly emphasized the futility of attempting to force people into a Christian mold of behavior through restrictions:

Why let people dictate to you: "Do not handle this, do not taste that, do not touch the other"—all of them things that must perish as soon as they are used? This is to follow merely human injunctions and teaching. True, it has an air of wisdom, with its forced piety, its self-mortification, and its severity to the body; *but it is of no use at all in combating sensuality.*

Were you not raised to life with Christ? Then aspire to the realm above, where Christ is, seated at the right hand of God, and let your thoughts dwell on that higher realm, not on this earthly life. . . .

Then put to death those parts of you which belong to the earth—fornication, indecency, lust, foul cravings, and the ruthless [sexual] greed which is nothing less than idolatry (Colossians 2:20b–3:1-2,5 NEB [emphasis mine]).

Any attempt to force conformance to a life-style of righteousness through religious laws will fail, unless there is an inner readiness of the heart to live in accordance with the will of Christ. The famous "don'ts" of Bible-belt fundamentalism—Don't smoke, don't dance, don't drink—seldom have any positive effect other than to solidify persons into a rigid self-righteousness that betrays their frustration over inner secrets of hypocrisy which cannot be shared without shattering their projected image of upstanding, moral respectability. Within, they are like living tombs "filled with dead persons' bones" (Matthew 23:27), for their lives have become manifestations of the lie of legalism.

God requires no more of us than an honesty of heart, coupled with a desire to do the will of Christ (Psalm 51:10; 40:8). It matters not how many times we may fail in our attempt to follow in the footsteps of Jesus; it *is* essential, as the writer of the book of Hebrews instructed, that we keep our eyes on the risen Lord and continue to contend for the infusion of the Holy Spirit's power within us. Then, by God's grace alone, we may be able to lead lives that are fully pleasing to the One who redeemed us with his own precious blood.

And what of ourselves? . . . We must throw off every encumbrance, every sin to which we cling, and run with resolution the race for which we are entered, our eyes fixed on Jesus, on whom faith depends from start to finish. . . .

> Think of him who submitted to such opposition from
> sinners: that will help you not to lose heart and grow
> faint. . . .
> Aim at peace with all men, and a holy life, for without
> that no one will see the Lord (Hebrews 12:1-2*a*, 3,14 NEB).

The reform of unredeemed patterns of human behavior can come
about only through a process of personal transformation inaugu-
rated by the Spirit of Jesus, for he is the One who convicts us of sin,
and convinces us of the need for righteousness and the certainty
of judgment (John 16:8-11). Thereafter, if we allow God to work
within us, the Spirit will begin to give us, through Christ's grace,
the ability to *purify ourselves* in accordance with the divine plan
for the ultimate perfection of the church:

> Everyone who has this hope before him purifies himself, as
> Christ is pure. . . .
> Such are the promises that have been made to us, dear
> friends. Let us therefore cleanse ourselves from all that can
> defile flesh or spirit, and in the fear of God complete our
> consecration (I John 3:3; II Corinthians 7:1 NEB).

According to the prophet Daniel (if we follow a futuristic interpretation of prophecy), in the closing days of this present age, just
before the return of Christ, "Many will be purged, purified and
refined; but the wicked will act wickedly, and none of the wicked
will understand, but those who have insight will understand"
(Daniel 12:10 NASV). To live a consistently Christian life-style in this
contemporary, hedonistically oriented society, a gay person needs
a spiritual insight that can be gained only through a personal
encounter with Jesus Christ. It is only through that keen perception that we are enabled to discern the highest of life's priorities, to
see beyond the transitory trivia and abusive self-indulgence that
engages a carnal culture. In order to live a life-style of moral purity,
we must rise above the herd mentality of the majority. We will
often be misunderstood, ridiculed, and rejected as we seriously
attempt to follow in the path of Christian discipleship, but it will
be our example that will cause others to question and probe their
own value-systems, in light of the hope of Christ they see radiating
from within us.

The risen Christ threatened to remove the lamp of spiritual

illumination from any church whose allegiance to the Lord is found to be wavering (Revelation 2:5). The gay Christian movement should reverently take heed, that it not be negligent in teaching a return to purifying holiness and Christ-centered life-styles, for any sidestepping of the issue can only result in a lack of spiritual perception and growth.

At this point in the progress of the gay religious movement, there is a great need for more ministers and lay people who, like the apostle Paul, will dare to declare the *whole* counsel of God (Acts 20:27) in areas of ethics and morality, as well as in the plan of salvation. The church is not here to enforce righteous life-styles on believers. The church is here, however, to proclaim in their entirety the New Testament exhortations concerning the proper expression of Christian living, including the general guidelines that are part of God's plan for our sexuality. When this has been done, the Holy Spirit will begin to move within the Body of Christ in our community, creating in gay believers a spirit of desiring obedience to the commandments of our Lord. When we begin to understand the working of God's sanctifying influence, it will become evident that the church is here to proclaim the gospel, while the Spirit works among us to bring forth a spontaneity of worship that will issue forth in obedience to the Word the church has spoken.

The message of Christ to the gay community is that he accepts and loves us just as we are, despite all our sins, failures, and confusion. "For at the very time when we were still powerless, then Christ died for the wicked. . . . Christ died for us while we were yet sinners, and that is God's own proof of his love towards us" (Romans 5:6, 8 NEB). But it is when we come to him in repentance, yielding him our allegiance, that the Lord Jesus, through the power of his Spirit, begins to change and transform us so that we may become *just as he is* (John 1:12; I John 2:6; 4:17).

Only as the gay Community of Faith is encouraged to become a living manifestation of the written Oracles of God—the only "Bible" many in the gay community will ever see—will we begin to be raised from one glorious level of living experience to another, until we reach that goal of becoming a radiant reflection of Jesus Christ (II Corinthians 3:18). This will result only when there is a revitalization and an increased emphasis upon the ministry of teaching, for without the food of apostolic guidance from the Scriptures, the deprived Body of Christ in the gay community will wither and die due to spiritual malnutrition.

Let us pray that a vision of holiness (human wholeness) will become a reality to those of us who are hungering for the *total* righteousness of Christ in the gay spiritual experience. However, this can come about only through discovering the beauty of a continual love affair with Jesus, our "First Love" (Revelation 2:4). Then our Christian pilgrimage will be transformed from a tedious effort, "trying to be good," to a liberating and joyous experience, as we yearn from the depths of our hearts to please the Lord, who is our ultimate, perfect Lover.

NOTES

1. Hans Jonas, *The Gnostic Religion: The Message of the Alien God and the Beginnings of Christianity*, (Boston: Beacon Press; 1963), pp. 274-75.
2. John R. W. Stott, *What Christ Thinks of the Church* (Grand Rapids: Wm. B. Eerdman's Publishing Co., 1958), pp. 71-72. Used by permission.
3. David B. Goodstein, "Opening Space," *The Advocate*, (March 18, 1982): 6.

Epilogue

It's hard being gay. It's harder yet to be a Christian. Some say it is impossible to be both at the same time. The existence of this book is an obvious indication that I do not agree with that declaration. But it is true that the struggle to be both gay and Christian is a call to sacrifice, alienation, and painful introspection. Visions of my past often rise from the deep mists of memory, vividly rekindling a journey of painful self-discovery. There were early adolescent years when one of my relatives would repeatedly tell me to "stop walking like a queer" because my gait did not seem to him to be masculine enough, not realizing that I suspected I was one of "them." After all, having a deeply romantic crush on Troy Donahue at age seventeen was not exactly living up to societal expectations for the red-blooded, all-American boy! But somehow, I naively expected those strange and unusual feelings to be a mere passing phase. It didn't pass.

At the time I was nine years old, God had become the central love and reality of my life, and throughout my years in high school, most of my spare time was spent reading the Bible and other varied theological writings. My faith was strong, if not sometimes overconfident.

Upon graduation, I began the agonizing struggle—coming to grips with the nature of my sexuality—which was not satisfactorily resolved until my mid-twenties. It was during that time that I tried many of the so-called deliverance techniques. I can vividly remember a Pentecostal woman writhing on the floor, "travailing in the Spirit" as she groaned in other tongues for my release from "homosexual demons"; after two hours, she pronounced me cured. It didn't work. I recall having the laying-on-of-hands administered during prayer by several prominent evangelical ministers who declared my deliverance from "perversion." They may have had famous reputations among the faithful, but on me, their hands just couldn't seem to convey the cure.

Of course, my limited understanding of Scripture at that time turned the reading of Romans 1 into a formidable confrontation between the contradictory forces of emotional trauma engendered by religious condemnation, and the emerging, inward certainty that my homosexuality was not alien to my natural self-expression. The mental anguish raged for years. It forced me to my knees in prayer, and it thrust me into a fray of confusion—sifting through the often conflicting theological and psychological literature on the subject of homosexuality.

"Coming out" into the gay community was an experience in itself, for it facilitated a final acceptance of myself and the inherent integrity of my sexual self-worth. Yet confusion continued to plague me. For example, my involvement with the Metropolitan Community Churches was a heightened faith-experience which served to cement my conviction that God loved me *as* a homosexual, rather than in spite of it. But the inconsistencies that I frequently observed between the Sunday-morning professions of faith and the subsequent behavior of numerous members began to disturb me to the extent that I questioned the validity either of the gay Christian experience, or of scriptural, Christian morality.

Gays Under Grace is the result of that long and arduous search for spiritual balance in the spheres of faith and morality. It is far from complete or finally definitive in its approach to homosexuality, the Bible, or the issue of Christian sexual ethics. But it is, at least, a modest attempt to raise a standard for truth, to begin to dispel the gross errors of prejudicial biblical interpretation.

Yet it is not the sole purpose of this book to make an academic, theological assault upon the bastions of the Moral Majority and its intolerant parochialism. At stake in the midst of this spiritual and social controversy are the many thousands of Christians who are "closet gays." Those people have a deep love for our Lord Jesus Christ. They are not immoral. In fact, many refuse to express their sexual inclinations in any overt manner because of the evangelical programming that has instilled in them the horrible misconception that to act upon their natural sexual inclinations would make them an "abomination" in the sight of God.

Unfortunately, many of those gay Christians have never been exposed to viewpoints that seek to explore homosexuality in a biblically responsible and psychologically positive manner. I hope this book will be yet another contribution to the spiritual illumination of those brothers and sisters in the Faith, who must endure their own private hells of sexual confusion and inner religious condemnation engendered by a wrongly programmed ethical conscience.

I know the agony of such experiences. I bear within myself the battle scars of mind and conscience, but what I have gone through is not unique, as the presently mute testimony of those sexually frustrated and mentally abused gay Christians will someday give witness. My message to them is a simple answer to the incessant, silent questioning, as they make a desperate attempt at self-understanding, and at the Spirit's understanding. . . . I know. I've been there. But I have progressed beyond the valley of confusion's shadows into the light of the Lord's liberty. . . . Listen to the Lord, to the One within. And most important, remember: To the extent that self is subject to the Spirit, "Above all, to thine own self be true."

Index To Scriptural References